UNIVERSAL REALITY

UNIVERSAL REALITY

PHYSICS
RELIGION
PSYCHOLOGY

HAROLD S. COBER

Harold Cober

LUTHERS
NEW SMYRNA BEACH

FIRST EDITION
Copyright © 1994 by Harold S. Cober
ALL RIGHTS RESERVED

Published by

LUTHERS
SAN: 200-3961   ISBN: 1-877633

1009 North Dixie Freeway
New Smyrna Beach, FL 32168-6221

PRINTED IN THE UNITED STATES OF AMERICA

LIBRARY OF CONGRESS
CATALOGING-IN-PUBLICATION DATA
Cober, Harold S., 1926–
Universal reality :
physics, religion, psychology /
Harold S. Cober — 1st ed.

p.   cm.
Includes bibliographical references.
ISBN 1-877633-23-2 (pbk.)
1. New Age movement.
2. Reality. 3. Psychology and religion.
I. Title.

BP605.N48C63 1994
299'.93 — dc20   94-31380
                                                CIP

A NOTE FROM THE AUTHOR

Since writing this book, I have determined that what I first identified as the Fifth Force is actually the *First Force*. It is the Source energy that everything is derived from. It travels at the *Ultimate Constant* speed which determines zero point.

I have also concluded that the sense of the First Force flowing through the human form, which at first appeared to be the sixth sense, should logically be called the *First Sense* (1s). The 1s must first ignite the reticular formation, the arousal center of the earth-brain, before the other five senses (5s) can be activated.

Harold Cober
Vibrational Religion Foundation, Universe
>religiousregistry.com/hcober<
The Institute of Technical Energy Medicine, Moscow
>item-bioenergy.com<
Research Director, Life Forces Research Fnd, Florida
>religiousregistry.com/hcober2020<
Keeper, Planetary Node #18

ABOUT THE COVER

Religion / Psychology / Physics

The cover depicts the energizing of the human brain. The yellow 'O's represent subatomic energy particles (Spirit). The yellow in the brain stem is the reticular formation (RF - soul) that causes the sensation of existence when ignited by these particles. The 'O' was selected to show that the energy field is complete for each individual, as opposed to a 'C' which would require a fusing of another entity for completion. The firmament is the carrier for energy particles as the atmosphere is the carrier for oxygen. The frontal lobe (FL) contains billions of synapses (see inset) which build circuits for thought and memory.

Reality is the sensation of the 'firing' of the reticular formation; *virtual reality* is extrinsic creations, by the synapses, of images which are perceptions of atom clusters (people, houses, cars, etc). These images are recorded in molecules (symbols pictured behind the brain) that materialize and dematerialize in the memory process.

Constituted or formed molecular structures (long term memory) are contained in *storage* and *virtual storage*. Storage is in the body system, probably in the ribonucleic acid (RNA). Virtual storage is spin-off memory molecules or vibrations that enter into the firmament (space). Virtual storage is the mechanism for non-verbal communication. This transition of molecules into the firmament can be seen as the aura surrounding a person's head (luminous radiation). The halo appears around certain people and is often pictured around Jesus.

Dedicated to

My wife, Nora
for being my resident critic
and research assistant.

The Author's quest for understanding life led to his decision to enter the ministry. After graduating from the University of Pittsburgh (with a degree in psychology) he came to a fork in the road. Instead of entering a religious seminary, he continued in postgraduate counseling courses at Frostburg College, Maryland. His career has been in Management Information Services. His first book, *The Rise of Man* was printed in 1993. A second book, *Man is Risen* was printed in 1994. He continues to write and give lectures. He resides in Daytona Beach, Florida.

TABLE OF CONTENTS

PREFACE x

Chapter I
    REALITY 1

Chapter II
    THE SIXTH SENSE 10

Chapter III
    THE FIFTH FORCE 15

Chapter IV
    INTELLIGENCE 22

Chapter V
    COSMIC ENERGY 28

Chapter VI
    BODY ENERGY SYSTEM 32

Chapter VII
    CELL REPAIR 36

Chapter VIII
    IDENTIFICATION 38

Chapter IX
    BEHAVIOR 40

Chapter X
    UNIVERSAL CONSCIOUSNESS 42

Chapter XI
    LOVE 47

Chapter XII
    MEDITATION 53

Chapter XIII
    VANISHING TRIBES 59

Chapter XIV
    THE REAL SECOND COMING 62

Chapter XV
    PROPHESY 65

Chapter XVI
    GOD'S WILL 68

NEW TESTAMENT II 73

REFERENCES 74

APPENDIX I 77

APPENDIX II 78

APPENDIX III 79

APPENDIX IV 80

APPENDIX V 81

ORDER FORM 83

PREFACE

The first book of my trilogy, *The Rise of Man,* discusses the development of consciousness and thought. It explains the evolution of the biosphere and the simultaneous involution of the noosphere. *Man is Risen,* discusses 'first cause' of consciousness and thought. It establishes an understanding of a Spiritual power *within* and implies that, since this power is eternal, man already is included in eternity. This book was written in that context.

The time has come to formulate a new NEW TESTAMENT. It will be a prescription, or formula, explaining the natural laws of living arrived at through physics, 'Apex Religion' and pure psychology. Its purpose is to enhance the expression of the Spirit. It will only legitimatize what "thou *shall*" do. A mass of information about how to live life exists today, but it is not understood or used by the masses. We have gone beyond guessing about the gods, and have found *"Him/Her"* to be the true reality within. It can be shown that the Spirit is the fifth force, and thereby it can be understood as we have learned to understand the other four. We no longer think of mind over matter because we now know that mind is matter. We know that reality is our sense of our soul, our sense of existence (consciousness) our sixth sense. We know that virtual reality is images, our perception of clumps of particles; i.e., money, power, etc. This gives new meaning to, "Thou shalt not put graven images before me."

A New Testament II is needed for the apex religion of the future. Youth can properly face a world community with a unified belief system; a system that has the same meaning and understanding for all nationalities. The Spirit within is the sameness shared by all human beings.

Today we know that everything in the universe is composed of dancing energy particles. The will of God is enacted by the attraction and repulsion of these particles. Thought is wave-like particles; memory is constituted particles, and health is particle symmetry. It is all set in motion, and follows natural laws, which provide us with the platform to understand the laws. Since particles follow natural laws, they must respond for the just and unjust alike. This explains why we can invent false gods and religions that exist only for acquiring health and wealth. Our *reason* for being is to locate the gift and adore the sense of "God particles" within us.

The true Spirit exists as an expression of God's image in man. The way to locate His image is to imprint on reality (existence) and put virtual reality (images) into perspective. This culminates in our pure adoration of His/Her presence within. *"The Second Coming"?*

Chapter I

REALITY

Defining reality is rather difficult. This author has researched the subject for over thirty years and, just now, feels comfortable sharing the findings. Some people have concluded that reality is whatever is *right for them*. This is superficial, because it lacks definition and understanding of natural laws. The word 'reality' is from the Latin "res" which comes from the verb "reri", which means *to think*. Pure thought, which is the sense of the moment, is pure reality. It *is* the *event,* not an interpretation of it. Reality is free of contradiction.

Real is 'what is'. It is *what is,* as opposed to what *seems* to be. Reality *is* the experience, not the image or interpretation of it. Reality is not a reflection like an apple or a billiard ball; it is an on-going process of pulsating cosmic stuff which cannot be distorted. It is not a static-standing-rigid 'something'. It is the energy flowing sense of *existing*. Descartes described consciousness as "thinking substance", which implies that it is not occurring in a void but rather it is interacting particles or energy fields. It is the on-going sense of energy fields igniting consciousness. Our sense of the divine is the sense of energy combustion prior to attitudes, judgment and even impressions.

In *The Celestine Prophecy* by James Redfield, it is said that the universe is a "...vast system of energy and that human conflict was a shortage of and a manipulation for this energy." We would add, not a shortage of the energy but a shortage of *knowledge* of sensing the energy. Consciousness does not exist in a void; it is not immaterial. It is the action of a unified energy field; it is real. It is "what is."

Virtual means 'not quite'. It is the image, the essence or effect of something, not the fact, as odor is the essence of perfume, not the perfume. Virtual is the *perceived* nature of something, a derivative, an image. What we see and interpret is the image of something. In the real world, *reality* is the sense of consciousness. *Virtual reality* is perceived images of our world. It is a camouflaged pattern, a derivative of the event. We have become so accustomed to mentally living in extrinsic institutions (virtual reality) that we expect to find our Supreme Power *out-there*.

A **noumenon** is what that 'something' is outside of our perception. A noumenon is what exists after consciousness is extinguished. It can not be known by human perceptual knowledge, so we can say that our version of what is 'out there' is a representation of the noumenon. Whatever comes to us is an image constructed by our perception of rearranging clusters of atoms. It is truly VIRTUAL reality.

Reality and virtual reality are the interaction of particles or force carrying particles. This is a wonderful arrangement because atoms follow preordained rules and do what atoms are supposed to do, regardless of what we expect them to do. Thought processes are merely the manipulation of atoms which follow laws. Natural laws can be understood and followed as we obey the law of gravity. With this knowledge, we can determine behavior just as we now track a hurricane, and understand it as a natural event. The great masters of physics have been the chief contributors to understanding these laws, but they are prohibited from leaving their discipline. They are not permitted to tell us how to use these laws in our conscious world. Religious theorists ought to take the findings of these great people and translate natural laws to the masses. So far, we have seen 'kinder-religion', which wastes time explaining what an individual must do in order to avoid retribution, rather than explaining what one must do to experience the joy of righteousness. These leaders attempt to explain God's mind instead of teaching how the individual can find the Spiritual laws within their own mind. Religious theorists should turn their heads from the past and help guide us to the future. Religion should be a step ahead of physics, psychology, sociology and physiology in idealism. By now, religion should have advanced mankind's understanding of how our brain functions at least beyond our knowledge of how computers function.

Most young people (and some old) know more about computers than they do about their own brain. Let us apply a small dose of physics and some logic. The brain contains the apparatus for *reality* and *virtual reality*. Reality is the sensation of ignition, caused by energy particles strumming the lower brain. Leon Lederman, in *The God Particle,* explains that "...all space, even empty space, is awash with particles, all that nature in her infinite wisdom can provide." The sensation of the particle energy conversion is 'what is' (reality). The sense of existence (consciousness) is the sensation of life before interpretation (virtual reality) 'kicks in'. The sense of existence is like 'cold' air; it cannot be seen but we certainly sense its presence. Waiting for the Spirit to come into our life is like waiting for oxygen to enter. It is already there.

Here we will go one step beyond physics to say, these particles or fields are 'Spiritual' particle-like energy. It is a definable driving force that exerts itself within the brain. It is the *soul* in man. True reality is the sense of this pulsating Spirit within which is God's image, the "Silver cord." The umbilical cord was our lifeline to this world; the Silver cord is our lifeline to the next. Virtual reality is the perception, by way of the synapses, of our outside environment. Symmetry and harmony are the result of recognizing reality first and then perceiving virtual reality. Today we live in reverse. We live as though we are 'planning' the trip of life instead of taking it. Reality, is 'experiencing' the cosmic erupting volcano within (consciousness). Virtual reality is 'seeing' an erupting volcano.

When on this trip, we should not mistake the map for the territory. Science provides the map; religion is part of the territory and should be the trip. Pure science in general, and physics in particular, is constructing the map. Religious leaders should be the tour guides. Instead, too often, they are merely historians of ancient ruins.

To experience *reality* is to experience the moment. In order to be 'on the trip', we must first have a sense of the 'engine' (the Spirit) firing within. Then we perceive *virtual reality* (the map) which is the perception of our environment. The engine drives consciousness and then we drive the synapses to form images. We control the latter but not the former.

Along with this wonderful driving force, our

Maker blessed us with unlimited **storage** (memory). There are two kinds of storage related to the brain, real storage (on-line) and virtual storage (off-line). Real storage is long-term memory molecules contained within the system. Virtual storage is memory particles contained in the medium firmament (space). We can assume that this grand process is driven by Spiritual energy. The proper use of the 'God supplied' process would produce the impetus for the "Second Coming." With this understanding, religion could have a whole new awakening.

There are universal applications for understanding the *Spirit within*. At the point of ignition, all human beings are equal. There are no male/female barriers because the Spirit is androgynous. There are no race barriers and no nationality barriers. We are all equal in that we all experience the same Spiritual particles within. Just as the same oxygen atoms allow breathing for all nationalities, the same subatomic particles allow consciousness for all.

As we move higher into the brain apparatus, we find the synapses that produce the circuitry responsible for virtual reality. They provide the mechanism for the other five senses. Here we are also equal in that there are no male or female synapses, no black, white, yellow, brown, no cowboy or Indian synapses or no superrace synapses. Some synapses function better than others, but that is determined by other factors.

It is important to understand that 'Cosmic Reality' applies to all human beings. Virtual reality is not the same for all people in all lands. Finding a common denominator that is the same for all, allows at least a starting point in understanding each other.

Reality gives an individual a solid base on which to stand. It allows a sense of security and confidence that is not shaken by "motives." These precarious motives are used when we attempt to protect the insecurities of virtual reality (race, nationality, drugs, etc.).

When one imprints on the Spirit within, virtual reality becomes secondary. It is still important but it is not foremost in one's existence. Insecurity is the most disquieting result of identifying with images. We often lose cars, houses, jobs, health and even people. Many times these losses put undue stress on the body system and one's behavior changes, even sickness and death can result. Reality does not change. Reality will not pay one's bills, but it can provide the source of strength to endure the losses and to continue earning a living.

Locating one's center or source of energy is not a retreat into oneself, but an active search for the inner-self.

Love of the inner-self must not be confused with narcissism. Narcissism is the love of the image one has conjured up for one's self. Individuals who are in love with their image suffer needlessly, because they are always attempting to prop up something that really does not exist. They are over-sensitive about their appearance and employ many ego-saving devices. The opposite of this is a negative self-image. This person experiences low self-esteem and suffers all of the anxieties that go with an inferiority complex. Many times, these are the bullies in society who are over-compensating. They push or coerce their way to the top in an effort to reinforce or 'prop up' a pseudo-existence.

The solution for both of these 'abnormalities' is to imprint on the Image of God within (the Spirit) and to transform the vitality of the universe into one's being. When this happens, no false images are created to interfere with being human. Aggression and anxiety just melt away.

Since man left the caves, almost everything he socially developed has been to conceal his inner being. Police provide protection; charities provide help in time of trouble, and insurance takes care of many emergencies. Lawyers have convinced people that everyone else is responsible for their client's mishap. Medicine indicates that cures exist in the pharmacy. All of these external forces tend to convince us that everything exists 'out-there'. A person cannot help but be alienated from his soul. It is important to remember that *we* divorce the Spirit; the Spirit *never* divorces us.

We begin life in the realm of reality. The infant has yet to learn about extrinsic images, but begins to construct them. The growth progression seems to skip reality and promotes development of virtual reality. In many cases, it reaches beyond virtual reality and into fantasy. Little is done to reverse the process. These layers of alienation can be measured by applying Karl Menninger's simple scale described in his book, *The Vital Balance* [see Appendix I]. The fifth and fourth order deals with fantasy, the third and second deal with virtual reality and the first order deals with reality. It becomes obvious that there is a natural law that alienation increases as we become more estranged from the Spirit. The reason for life is to locate that center. The purpose is to adore, accentuate and enhance that center.

Living only in virtual reality and beyond is the experienced shortage and manipulation of the fifth force (Spiritual energy) as expressed by James Redfield. In search of 'real' security, we settle for 'pseudo-security' in appendages (virtual reality); i.e., things, institutions, people. We attempt to get this security by manipulating these images. The ultimate attempt to steal this energy is murder.

A new New Testament (detailed later) would give us the knowledge to recognize the energy field within. We mention here that, as in all of nature, when attaining the energy that is available to all, a curve develops. The true learning curve climbs the scale as one begins new learning, then reaches a plateau and declines. However, as learning continues, the curve (amount learned) again climbs higher than the last plateau. Attaining the first order (reality) follows this rule. One first begins to sense the "Spirit-titre", as described in Sidney J. Jourard's *The Transparent Self*, and then the sense of it subsides temporarily only to return stronger. Each level advances to a higher level.

Reality or consciousness is what unites humans. It is sensing the eternal Spirit. Some cultures believe there are many spirits and that spirits reside in all of nature. The particle-like theory of the Spirit shows us that there is only one force energizing *us* as well as everything else in the universe. As we all intake oxygen from the air, we all intake subatomic particles from one universal energy field.

Yogi Berra once said, "If you come to a fork in the road, take it." Reality is the road before the fork. It is our existence before we construct mental images. Virtual reality extends beyond the forks, and fantasy is beyond the forks and into a maze. Human development prematurely forces us into the forks in the road before we have experienced the main highway. Our identity becomes an alliance with constructed images and we succumb to forces that do not exist. To be mentally reborn is regaining a sense of the main highway (feel the energy within) and then identifying the forks (extrinsic images). It is difficult to 'let go' of images that have become our identity and to imprint the Spirit. By this time, we think that we *are* the images and, if we let go, we might cease to exist. The opposite is true; letting go of these images is the beginning of true existence.

Chapter II

THE SIXTH SENSE

We fail to recognize what is real. This causes us to live equivalent to enjoying pictures of ice cream instead of savouring it with our sense of taste. True 'reality' is *experiencing* our existence at the *moment*. The five senses give us virtual pictures but we seem to have missed the most important sense, the SENSE OF EXISTENCE. This is the **sixth sense** and it is the 'engine' that drives the other five. (Not to be confused with a sixth sense that some have attributed to ESP.) The real sixth sense is the most important and should have been understood before the other five senses. It is the one that tells us we are alive. Something triggers this sixth sense, just as something must jiggle our olfactory nerves to allow us to experience the sense of smell. We are not self-igniting. Something has to strike the match.

In order to understand the sixth sense and what drives it, we will take a quick look at subatomic particles. They appear to work like little universes. They explode, give off energy, collapse and then fire again (as in big bang, red shift and black hole). This is a never ending cycle. Consciousness is our sense of these subatomic nano-explosions firing the brain. Light waves jiggle receptors and cause images on our sense of sight. Subatomic energy 'jiggles' the reticular formation of the brain, initiates life, and causes the sensation of consciousness.

Consciousness gives the impression of a steady flow of awareness. If the energy that powers the brain is, as Einstein described light waves, "a steady stream of bullets", how can we sense an *even* flow of consciousness? Photons fool the brain just as a lot of other stimuli fool the brain. When a series of still pictures pass before our eyes, our sense of sight sees it as continuous, unbroken movement. As sound vibrations bombard the auditory system, we hear a continuous flow of music. As the cosmic rhythmic energy (God particle, as described by Leon Lederman?) strikes and fires the receptors in the brain stem, we experience an *even flow* of consciousness.

As oxygen atoms enter the lungs and allow us to breathe, subatomic wave-like particles enter the lower brain stem and allow the sensation of existing. From there a chain reaction is set in motion to power our senses, thought and memory. We cannot 'see' oxygen atoms or subatomic particles but, as in Einstein's example of the watch, we can apply the law of probability. We can determine, without looking inside the watch, that something coordinates the hands. Those who lack the ability to conceptualize will say probability proves nothing. Would insurance companies discontinue using statistics to determine how many people will die next year because they cannot predict *who* will die? When natural laws are revealed, with the use of scientific methods of probability, we must agree that there is something going on inside the watch. We will someday see the thought process in the 'case' but, for now, we can only look for 'fingerprints'. Consciousness is a fingerprint of subatomic action.

Consciousness is not under our control. We cannot decide to be conscious or not conscious (without taking one's life and even then, who knows). Beyond this we do have control. We are in charge of thought and memory. These gifts, too, exhibit fingerprints of waves and particles. Thought is *not* ethereal and lacking structure. Thoughts are electrical waves or wave-like particles, similar to short term memory. Long term memory is constituted subatomic particles. It is conceived constructs of particles materializing (coding), dematerializing, and then reconstituting for recall (decoding). Nonverbal communication is not an exact science but it can be demonstrated. The way it occurs is the brain codes and decodes waves, or virtual particles, which 'ripple' in the firmament. Brains transmit 'data signals' as do satellite dishes. Most signals are scrambled but it is just possible that the 'Superbrain' has the black box.

Because we have not learned to experience our sixth sense as we have the other five, we attempt to imprint or find an identity 'out-there'. We attempt to find reality in 'virtual reality', in a picture of ourselves instead of experiencing ourselves. Reality is the sense of exploding subatoms in the lower brain, and everything beyond that is an image (virtual reality). "Thou shalt not make unto thee any graven image...." Graven not only means to carve or shape a solid, but also to impress or fix as a thought.

The structure of thought and memory seems to react like subatomic structures. When an attempt is made to view the electron clouds around the nucleus of an atom, the property is affected by the instrument used to 'see' it. To examine an idea, the shell or layer of belief around the nucleus of consciousness changes the characteristics of the idea. As a prism refracts light, layers of prior 'beliefs' disperse or refract the idea. Richard W. Wetherill, in *Emergence of Ratio-*

nality, identifies these layers or appendages as "motives." Rational thought or true verbal communication cannot take place through these motives. Our government suffers from this malady. After election, how can an issue be openly examined by refracting it through the shell of biased thinking as a Republican or a Democrat? How can we communicate with other human beings by refracting thoughts through nationalism, patriotism or racism?

To demonstrate this law, we will make the statement, "CHRIST is a principle that existed in the world prior to Jesus." Suppose subject 'A' had no shell or construct of Jesus (never heard of Him). 'A' could study the concept of the statement freely. Subject 'B', having heard that Jesus brought 'the Christ' into the world, would hardly examine the statement without a motive (an open mind). Subject 'C', having pseudo-imprinted on that shell, would probably close shop and would not even examine the proposition.

The natural law of reality dictates that one sense the center of one's existence. The further one strays from reality, the more fragmented and unstable that person becomes. There are two methods of quantifying stability. The *first* one is using Menninger's five orders of dyscontrol as described in *The Rise of Man*. It simply, by degree, locates where one is on the scale. The location is determined by how fragmented a person's nucleus is, and by the strength of that identity with outer shells or appendages. A person in the first order does not use motives, and would deal with life from pure reality. The second order might be one who vacillates between reality and virtual reality. Farther down the scale, we find the Mansons who live far beyond virtual reality.

The *second* method (described in *Man is Risen*) is similar but uses the Spiritual Influence Table. Since the soul is the seat of consciousness, the sixth sense is simply Spiritual energy particles bombarding the area of the brain stem. This causes one to sense life (reality). It borrows from Meninger's scale and measures how far one has strayed from the Spirit within. The first order would include all of those who have imprinted on the Spirit and are no longer confused by virtual reality. If man is to fulfill the "Second Coming", the masses need to find their way to the first order.

To locate and imprint on the Spirit within, one needs to understand 'proximal distal' mental development (*Man is Risen*). It is to be mentally reborn, to imprint on the Spirit, and then to identify virtual reality (appendages). Baptism should be a symbol that this conversion has taken place, in fact, as opposed to what is today's misinterpretation. It should be seen as a rite of passage. Anabaptism might be recommended because the conversion can only occur after appropriate training.

Chapter III

THE FIFTH FORCE

There are four categories of known forces in the universe: gravity, electro-magnetic, weak atomic and strong atomic. These forces usually fit into a mechanistic particle theory, but in order to locate the ultimate building block, it might be necessary to think of the 'building block' as a unified energy field (sub-atomic crazy glue). In order to study the universe, it is easier to look at each part and then we begin to see the universe as a collection of related parts. Nothing is a *part* in the universe, it is all one organism. We cannot, for example, think our skin sets us apart; it is a screened window through which subatomic particle-like energy flows as it does through trees and galaxies.

We are looking for the "God particle." In this context, God is not used in the sense of early man's traditional view as an unknowable father figure. Rather it is used as the knowable ultimate energy process, a force field. It might not necessarily be a particle but self-perpetuating energy, a "God Principle." We need not know the detail of these studies in order to know that whatever it is, it is an entity that follows natural laws. It is not necessary to know the chemical formula for antifreeze to know it keeps water from freezing. We will one day totally understand the force field because, as everything else in the universe, it follows patterns of order and measure.

In order to give meaning to this power source, we will identify it as **'the fifth force'**. We should not think of these forces as a hierarchy, but rather they are numbered in the order discovered. The 'fifth force' is actually the "first cause" in the other four and is in all organic and inorganic structures. It makes sense to understand it as a unified force field which pulsates energy and drives the other forces in the universe. As the macrocosm big bang, unfoldment, and black hole continually regenerate the universe (as if the universe were breathing) so does the microcosm fifth force field collide, release energy and disappear. Constructive thinking follows the same law and manipulates energy substance as questioning, intuiting and answering.

The significance of this discussion is to understand that the fifth force drives consciousness and the cosmos. It can be quantified as we do all other forces. There is one 'God Force Field' and it is integrated into one universal, unified energy system. Eastern religion and philosophy has always accepted this idea because they observed it in action. The West is arriving at the same conclusion by a totally different route, science. The East knows that it works, the West will one day know *how* it works. It is difficult to separate fact from imagination in the Eastern version. If one claims the chair fell over because the bird chirped, we lose the skeptics. If one observes energy transition on a scope, it is a proven happening. A unified understanding of Spiritual energy follows the laws of energy and can be demonstrated. The fifth force has nothing to do with what we believe; it has to do with 'what is'. It does not require faith, belief or dogma any more than it would require these agents to know that there is a Mt. Rushmore.

It is interesting to note that some researchers

believe that communication is possible within the energy field. There is communication between the atoms in the brain and the atoms in the immune system. There is atomic communication when resting atoms fire-up, to retard the chemicals that keep us awake and allow sleep. One could say that the reticular formation is required for the translation of consciousness in the physical body, but the translation can be carried on in the fifth force field. This process is partially at work while we sleep, and explains out-of-body experiences, and perhaps eternal life.

The survival of mankind ultimately may depend on understanding the fifth force. There is no hard evidence to show that there is anything other than the fifth force field propelling the universe and life. While we wait for a 'man devised' GOD to act, we waste precious time to do what we know must be done, which is to live righteously. Mature behavior depends, first, on recognizing *reality*. Reality is experiencing the cosmic pulsating force field 'firing' the brain. Second, on recognizing *virtual reality* we form constructs which are the direct result of this energy being manipulated by our intent. We human beings use pure energy to form false constructs, and then believe these images are reality. We negatively respond to forces that do not exist. We worship virtual reality instead of the Spirit. The misuse of energy results in conflict.

With this new understanding of the fifth force, it is time for a *new* "New Testament." New Testament II will enlighten and teach ways to embody the Christ principle as discussed in *Man is Risen*. It will show mankind a truth that would support the Second Coming (people living as Jesus and other righteous scholars have taught). It will promote good, not out of fear of reprisal for doing wrong, but for the satisfaction of doing right. It will only define 'good' thereby not legitimatizing wrong. It will be a framework of changing ideas, rather than fixed rules and regulations. We need to face the fact that, since the Spirit is *only* the propellant, it is up to us to accept the *responsibility* for protecting our internal and external environment.

Our first responsibility is to remove appendages which cause wars and destruction. There is no need to invent false images (appendages) when one imprints the soul. [Appendix I depicts levels of behavioral dyscontrol.] To live in reality is to establish one's identity in the first order. To find one's identity in any of the other orders is to worship false gods. Again, this does not mean we must rid ourselves of possessions, we need only change our perspective. It means to first imprint on our being and then to identify possessions. Possessions can be more meaningful when they do not *own* us.

We have been told we cannot have good without the contrast of 'bad'. We are conditioned to think that, since there is a God, there must be a devil. Good and bad cannot exist simultaneously. Man cannot think *good* and *bad*; he must select one or the other. This idea of contrast is a false assumption because evil does not exist when living the Christ principle (first order). We need to transcend the illusion, form true constructs, and live in reality (a pure mind set). The 'grand hallucination' is to form false constructs.

Some writers use the excuse that false form is necessary to attain righteousness. They tell us that in order for us to gain moral strength adversity is required. Must we first wreck a car in order to learn how to drive? Sometimes, overcoming adversity can contribute to strength, but it is not the prerequisite. What we lack is a formula explaining how to attain strength directly from the Spirit.

It is folly to think we have to contrast good and evil. We only do this because we lack definition of good and expect to find it by isolating evil. This new experiment suggests that there is only good and that we conjure up evil. The new New Testament will teach that there is a formula for good that each person can follow. It is that simple! New Testament II will not rely on subjective thought to determine good. Good will be measured. It is not difficult to recognize right thought and behavior because it brings about symmetry of the atoms in the body (David Bohm, *Wholeness and the Implicate Order*). As a true chord on a musical instrument creates resonance and harmony of sound waves, so does true thought create symmetry, and order, of energy fields in the body and in the world.

We are now 'off key'. It is interesting to note that it is no sin to play an instrument off key; it is just annoying. The solution for the beginner is to practice until he/she gets it right. Likewise, 'out of tune' behavior is not a sin, just ignorance of the natural law of behavior. There are tuning forks to show when a note is in tune. We will one day have a tuning fork to tell when our thoughts are in tune. Our brain is already capable of telling us this, but we have not yet learned to sense resonance. Biofeedback comes close to this endeavor, but it is far removed from body synchronization. False form is behavior out of harmony; true form is cognitive consonance. There is no need to waste time to study false form in order to eliminate it. All we need do is identify the symmetry of true form and practice it. False form will not exist when we learn to understand and practice true form.

New Testament II will be based on natural laws of energy and what appears on the scope. It will never be complete because we will forever be locating new laws and new understandings of energy. It will continue to reflect the work of the great men and women of science who study it from both ends of the 'funnel'. It will use both the explicate and the implicate (David Bohm) approach to a knowledge of our *being*. We need to begin to apply the knowledge of the explicate order we gain from instruments like the Hubble telescope. What does it mean to mankind to understand 'black holes' and the discovery of water 200 million light years away? The implicate order is 'seen' with tunneling microscopes and accelerators by which we have just now (1994) located the "top quark." There are many more levels of energy in the universe to be understood. The Old Testament closed the period on man's social infancy. The New Testament closed the period on man's social teen years, but New Testament II will not close because man/woman will continue to mentally mature. The consciousness of the Spirit will continue to intensify and express itself.

The past is important but it never explains how atoms function in our body, what consciousness is, how the brain communicates with the immune system, how memory works, how we mentally construct graven images or how body symmetry is maintained. Our future depends on understanding all of these things. Telling a drug addict that God once punished the world with a flood does little to change his/her habit. It does more good to explain what the drug is doing to body cells and teach how to imprint on the real power within (first order) as opposed to identifying with extrinsic false gods [fourth order — Appendix I].

Energy of the fifth force is to the body as electricity is to a city. Electricity will light a city or, when out of phase, will burn down your house. When in phase, the fifth force will power your body, but out of phase it will destroy you. The fifth force drives every particle, molecule, cell and synapse in our body while powering the universe. It is all the same energy. The new New Testament will not threaten or coerce. It will merely explain the natural laws of thought, so we can observe and respect them as we now observe and obey gravity.

Chapter IV

INTELLIGENCE

All life can be seen as a self-perpetuating cycle, which observes natural laws. When we understand the dynamics of this cycle in the universe there is one process that emerges. Within the never-ending expanse, we see continual big bangs, red shifts and black holes. We see it in the seed, flowering and decaying; birth, maturation and death. We sense it in consciousness. Within all of this, or because of all of this, we can detect the flow of energy fields. This particle-like energy will be *seen* on devices like the Superconductor Super Collider, but for now, it can only be demonstrated and understood heuristically (with the use of informed common sense).

We can observe this particle-like flow in an ontological look at the human brain. A human's existence begins with this energy flowing across, and igniting, the reticular formation in the lower brain (soul). Why is it taking so long for this to be accepted? In the fifth century B.C., Democritus said, "Fire is composed of small, spherical atoms, as is the soul of man." Consciousness is the sensation derived from atomic nano-explosions. This is *being* itself, before we corrupt or contaminate it into constituted molecular structures (memory, engrams, memes).

The flow of subatomic particles (raw energy) into, or through, the brain gives no direction or guidance. That is our responsibility. We now use this awesome power as though we are the source. Our job is to understand the natural law of this power and use it to construct true forms. Here is the port of entry for free will. We are permitted to create false forms, but it is as fatal as not following the law of gravity.

The upper brain is the 'engram pump', or processor, responsible for thought and memory. By one's *intent* and nature's 'chemical explosions', we form engrams and memory traces. Thought is meta-waves and memory is meta-particles. The molecular structures we form (constructs) are dependent on our intent and interpretation through our limited senses. One of the most important discoveries of the century is the particle theory of the *mind*. Few seem to realize that until thought is understood to behave within natural laws, *reality* and behavior are relative. We know of nothing that is outside natural law and thought is no exception.

Beyond consciousness, all brain function is dependent upon on/off switches (synapses), which are bathed in electro-chemical juices. The synapse is man's greatest possession. Brain function is not caused by a continuous flow of electricity through nerve pathways. If it where, we would not be much more than a punch card. Instead, there are gaps in the pathways that are bridged by an electro-bath. This is what allows us to make good decisions and mistakes (free will). The distance and the speed these *signals* travel are totally dependent on the billions of switches and the intent of the author (you). Because the 'potassium pump' has an on/off switch, there is a time for the synapse to *fire* and a time for *rest* (reverse polarity). A simple way to put it is, the switch is turned **on** (polarized) by acetylcholine and turned **off** (depolarized) by the influx of acetylcholinesterase. Steven Rose (*The Making of Memory*) states "Nerve cell activity is electrical, and biologically generated current (which) flows through the brain in patterns as simultaneously regular and varied as the waves of the sea."

This information has no practical purpose until we learn to apply it to human behavior. One application is to acquire intelligence. All learning (discounting intent, discussed later) is dependent on these switches. We could call this 'native intelligence'. By using a method like the SQUID (super-conducting quantum interference device) that Rose describes, we can detect tiny magnetic fields, no larger than one billionth of the earth's magnetic field. If it could be determined, by this or some other method for example, that a healthy switch fires in .005 millionth of a nanosecond, we could measure true native intelligence. If a subject's synapse time would measure .004, we could be sure that person would not learn as quickly as one who measures .005. Healthy switches carry the proper current, through the proper pathways, to a point where engrams are formed and molecular structures are constituted. Unhealthy switches slow or stop the process. Over-loaded switches (bioplasmic spill-over) also interfere with learning. Proper uses of these pathways (learning) create more pathways, which allow more pathways to develop.

Conventional methods of testing "IQ" (intelligence quotient) tells us very little about a person. They merely show one's exposure to facts. If one lives in a house and is asked about a door knob, he/she can show a high IQ. If one is raised in a cave and is asked about a door knob, he/she will show a low IQ: yet the two subjects may both measure the same native intelligence of .005.

This synapse time should be totally understood by care-givers in order to properly teach children. If a child's synapse time is .004 and they expect that child to learn at the same rate as the .005 child, they will probably create a dropout. If they expect the .005 to learn at the same rate as the .004, they will create boredom and again perhaps a dropout. The important thing to know is that both have the ability to assimilate the same number of facts, but at a different rate.

In the near future there will be a little instrument invented, like a thermometer, that can measure synapse time through the ear or eye. We could discover if certain foods effected the time, or if certain mental gymnastics improved the time. Neuroscientists, like Lawrence Farwell, can detect when a person is lying by putting a small band on the head and recording a "mermer". Surely this is *reading* synapses and lends to the thought that we will one day be able to detect synapse time itself.

The only complicated faction involved in the process is the user's intention. We can increase the magnitude of the switches by our intention or desire. A high achiever could be a normally motivated .005 or a highly motivated .004. Of course the reverse of this is true. My heart goes out to the .035 child whose care-givers think he/she is a .005. My sympathy goes out to the .005 child who thinks, or has been convinced, that he/she is a .035.

We can only speculate how young people would learn to handle drugs or alcohol if they realized, in fact, how these chemicals damage their *switches*. The firing of a synapse is based solely on proper chemical balance. It is proven that when toxic chemicals are introduced to the body, the chemical balance is permanently damaged whether the user believes it or not.

"Eidetic imagery" is voluntary production of memory that records and recalls mental images having almost photographic accuracy. We have known about eidetic memory for a long time, but Rose points out, that in follow-up studies, it is found to be more prevalent than first believed. It occurs most frequently before puberty. How sad if schools or parents destroy it! Using our native intelligence scale, perhaps an individual with eidetic memory will register a synapse time of .006. Perhaps with understanding, we could develop more .006s. It is just possible that we all started as 006s and were misguided. This kind of memory has a down side; some of these people *cannot* forget. It seems possible that they could be *taught* to disconnect from storage.

Hybrid memory favors no sex or race. This lends support to Cober's theory that there are no girl synapses and no boy synapses, merely **synapses**. At this level of the brain, before we clutter it with preordained opinions, neither sex nor race is favored. Energy particles are androgynous and colorless.

Memory can be classified in two groups, natural and artificial. Natural memory includes short and long term (discussed earlier) and is dynamic and continually changing. Artificial memory is written, or typed, and remains fixed. Word processors begin to push the boundaries of artificial memory because, while on-line, the printed text can be edited.

If parts of our brain operate similar to personal computers, we should be able to understand non-verbal communication. Personal computers network all over the world. Are we not equipped to 'network' other *brains?*

The real danger in relying on non-verbal communication through sub-atomic particles, or light patterns, is in understanding the difference between selfish desires and true communication. Is the received 'message' something we are constructing? Is it something we *imagine* we are 'picking-up', or is it a true transmission? One day, we will learn to know the difference. Personally, I have not 'tuned-in' to any of these transmissions, but have little doubt that they do occur.

Chapter V

COSMIC ENERGY

The sensation of personal existence (consciousness) is the perception of nano-explosions in the brain stem (reticular formation). It is the sense of an energy conversion. It is probably not sensed by the plant in photosynthesis, and is not sensed in the auto engine, but it is surely sensed in the human brain. Energy particles ignite the brain *engine* which allows us to sense our being. At this juncture of the energy cone, there are no preordained or preconceived ideas and, especially, there are no bicameral thoughts (messages from the gods). It is simply experiencing our existence (reality). With this power source from the lower brain, we learn to manipulate the synapses in the upper brain (frontal lobe). As an infant, we begin with a tabula raza (blank slate) and are free to form or constitute virtual reality. We cannot affect the strength of the energy within, but we can learn to recognize and intensify the feeling.

With the recognition of near death experiences, the seat of the soul (location in the brain) has again come into speculation. NDEs seem to occur in the "Sylvian fissure" and some have suggested this might be the soul. We agree with the first publication of *The Transparent Self* by Sidney M. Jourard, where he indicated the "Spirit-titre" might be found in the reticular formation. There is no question that consciousness occurs in the lower brain. The Sylvian fissure is located higher and could come into play when the brain is powered down, but it is not the sole manufacturer of hallucinations.

Cosmic energy is now unknown subatomic particle-like substance or a unified energy field, but it does leave 'fingerprints' everywhere. Physicists will one-day unveil the "God Particle" or energy cloud. It will also require endocrinologists and neuroscientists and a lot of other disciplines working together to uncover this Holy Grail. The problem now is, as stated by Dr. Felten, "They would rather use each others tooth brushes than work together." Candice Pert, Ph.D., in Bill Moyer's book *Healing and the Mind* said, "...clearly there is another form of energy that we have not yet understood." As everything else in nature it will turn out to be quite simple and beautiful. There will be those who say, "I knew that." Cosmic energy will probably be classified as the 'fifth force'. It will be found to be the fuel that fires the human brain accounting for the real sixth sense, the sense of existence.

The power source can be seen as spiritual and the point of ignition in the human is his/her soul. This is the only pure reality we can ever know. There is an observable tropism toward this center of our being. The natural state of the brain is wellness. Except for isolated cases, the brain is set to accept truth in its environment. Other than the few instances of molecular failures, we are responsible for keeping out the garbage (fantasies).

We are in complete control after the fire is started in our brain. The lower portion has some autonomic assignments but the top is ours. We have been given complete free will. From this point on, we have the right to understand or *misunderstand* our environment, even our very existence. We have the right to destroy our brain or to keep it healthy. We can energize righteousness or legitimatize wickedness. Moral weakness is merely the absence of knowledge of our inner strength.

Most of us fail to recognize our power source and lack confidence in the engine. We invent things and practice "control drama" to alter our states of consciousness. Jean Paul Sarte, in his complicated book *Being and Nothingness,* holds that everything man mentally does, is done to enhance his sense of existence. His fear of nothingness (not being) creates inner emptiness that drives him to continually reinforce his fictitious sense of being. Sarte believed these negative devices ranged from the use of drugs to waging wars.

Dr. Menninger in *The Vital Balance* wrote, the trick to mental health is to attempt to remain on the "bubble." Autism is the failure or inability to manipulate the upper brain; hyperactivity is the misuse or abuse of it. The homeostasis of the brain (nano-thermostats) strives for equilibrium. The natural state of the brain is to attain cognitive consonance. Every molecule, atom, quark or Higgs particle responds to its environment. If the brain's existence is threatened by danger, or perceived danger, cognitive dissonance occurs. The nano-thermostats call in the juices so the body can fight or take flight.

When these extra juices are flowing into the synapses, it gives one a feeling of exhilaration and thereby reinforces one's sense of existence. If the threat is real and then subsides, the engine returns to normal. The heightened sense of awareness is dulled and to some it is akin to not-being. There are those who will take synthetic juice (drugs) in an attempt to return to a higher state of arousal. Some achieve this heightened sense through horror movies, but others argue, fight, rob, rape or kill. This is the autotelic principle run amok. Like all addiction, the habit must be continually reinforced and increased. Continual overflow of these juices causes fatigue in the synapse and the brain circuits break down; illness often follows.

Chapter VI

BODY ENERGY SYSTEM

Most of the human body systems are well known. We know about food digestion, blood circulation, the nervous system, etc. Our energy system is less known but it is by far the most important. The energy distribution system must be intact in order to drive the others. We know so little about our energy system because it is made up of subatomic energy particles (the fifth force) that have not yet been 'seen' by physicists. Of course we see the food we take in and burn. We know that we take in and burn oxygen, but it is difficult to 'see' the energy particles bombarding the body.

The energy system and the autonomic nervous system are similar. The autonomic nervous system is the unit that regulates our body functions (heartbeat) while allowing the brain to handle more pressing problems. One part of the system activates impulses to the body (sympathetic) while the other inhibits these impulses (parasympathic). Many years ago it was believed that the autonomic system operated independent of our thoughts. Today we know we can affect it but that it functions best when we *mentally* do not interfere.

The energy system is a dimension of personal existence. It is automatic in that it flows through us without our beseeching it or, as in most cases, without our perception of it. Some might believe that it operates independently of our control; in fact, we have studies that prove we can intervene. Like the sympathetic and parasympathetic it strives for symmetry and does best when mentally not disturbed.

What do we mean by *mental* interference? The proper state of this energy (the fifth force) enters the brain stem and excites the neurons (the sixth sense) in that order. Cosmic order dictates that these energy particles carry out their preordained instructions. Sympathetic energy ignites cells and parasympathetic energy keeps them in check. Hyperactivity, bioplasmic spill-over or "sparking over" is caused by excessive flow. Autism is the opposite extreme. In a very few cases these extremes are genetic, but in the vast majority, it is mental manipulation that causes the imbalance. Because of improper thought processes, the "vital balance" of energy collapses; it is mental interference.

Man's true state is to, first, sense *being* itself and then to experience his outer world. The inner sense can be viewed as raw energy or as Spiritual energy. In either case, the further one mentally strays from center (soul) the greater the sense of alienation. One becomes toxic. Living in reality effects endorphins, cortosol and maybe even cholesterol. We can diagram this and show that five orders of alienation exist. The first order is imprinting on pure reality. It is the closest to the 'light' man can attain on this plane. The second and third order are to identify our being as virtual reality, *images* of who we think we are. The fourth and fifth order are to go beyond virtual reality and enter into fantasy. This can be seen when people become obsessed or mentally identify with an image (girl friend, wife, job) and will kill rather than give up that image. They have lost the sense of themselves. They only exist through an image, and if the image is removed they believe they will cease to exist.

The fourth and fifth orders are the extreme but dissonance can occur in the second and third. One can heavily identify with virtual reality and, when that image is threatened, the sense of existence is threatened. The resulting anxiety disrupts the natural flow of energy, because the energy shifts to the fight or flight organs, and particle symmetry is disrupted. More illnesses can occur in the second and third order because in the fourth and fifth the person no longer senses danger.

We have discussed appendages or mental baggage that we acquire. As we grow, we begin to identify with other people, things or organizations. Illness can occur when these false gods are threatened or lost. We can then add 'illness' to the appendage list. People who have a disease, or think they have a disease, begin to believe they *are the disease*. Their life centers around the illness and they pseudo-imprint on the illness. This legitimatizes the illness even if it is an organic disease.

Much has been written about positive thinking and 'willing' oneself well, but that simply wastes more energy. In order to utilize the never-ending energy particles afforded us, all we need do is *not* hinder their flow. Cognitive consonance is attained by imprinting on the Spiritual power within and allowing the pharmacy in the brain to do what it was designed to do. This body energy system is as dependable as all other natural laws. It will function when mental symmetry is attained. It does not depend on beliefs.

If there is evil behavior, it is diminishing or depleting another's Spirit-titre. Our reason for being is to experience and exemplify the supreme Spirit in ourselves and in others. We have a responsibility to others to assist in strengthening their being. Teachers and parents should be mindful that it is their responsibility not only to teach but to allow the *inner child* to develop. We cannot destroy the Supreme Energy. We can stifle it within ourselves and others.

Chapter VII

CELL REPAIR

Ultimately, all healing begins at the cellular level. Healing is a collective ballet of cells. Even "miracle cures" do not occur outside of cell structure. Cells can only do what cells were designed to do. Cure, by any means, restores rhythm to the atomic 'dance'. These cells do not work independently of our free will, and we can interfere with the symmetry by thought interference.

The way we perceive our sickness affects our illness. David Felton, M.D., Ph.D. at the University of Rochester School of Medicine, has found a direct physical link between the brain and the immune system. For years, it has been suggested that we have some control over our immune system but, until Dr. Felton's discovery, it could not be proven.

Everything that happens to the body draws from the pharmacy of the brain. The brain sends out neurotransmitters. The body receives the messenger molecules with its cell receptors and messages are returned to the brain. Only when the body is in symmetry does this orchestration function as designed. Symmetry is acquired by centering or focusing our *mind* on one thought. Perfect symmetry is attained when focusing on the sense of the *one* Spirit within. When one learns to focus on the power within, symmetry or resonance occurs in the body and the immune system returns to full strength.

The flu or a cold can appear quickly after the onset of an emotional disturbance. Sometimes a more serious upset causes damage to the immune system and it can be a rather slow process. This is like polluting a lake; it takes time to pollute and therefore it takes time to clear. Except in rare cases, even after one learns to properly use the mind, it can take months and years to 'unpollute'. The immune system seems to deteriorate with age. One wonders if the cause is just age or prolonged disruption by unreal stress.

One can see the tremendous power emotions exert on cells. Dr. Pert points out that people with multiple personalities will display a different illness for each personality type. Certainly this indicates how one can disrupt health. Seeing this, some feel that the solution to health is to 'visualize' or make a 'request' for health. If this were true, how do we account for an infant's health? An infant has not yet learned to make 'requests' or to think 'health'. However, an infant has not yet learned to mentally interfere with its body transmitters and receptors. This leads me to believe that the answer is to understand the cosmic flow (in fact) and to have confidence in it. Nothing seems to cause disruption of services more than an attempt to manipulate or coerce cellular action. The solution lies more with damage control than with health control.

Chapter VIII

IDENTIFICATION

Base-line consciousness is the sense of existence prior to the layering or build-up of constituted molecular structures (recorded symbols). This is merely experiencing the nano-explosions of our soul being energized by spiritual energy particles. At this level we have no concern with identity; we have only the sense of the Spirit within.

In order to obtain an identity, the synapses fire and the reverberating circuits of the brain begin to form memory traces. This is imprinting. Animal imprinting is fixed to record whatever is audible and/or visual at a set time after birth. Animal imprinting is irreversible.

Man begins to imprint when the upper circuits in the brain begin to fire. This is pseudo-imprinting, because the first recorded impressions are false. They are extraneous impressions of who we are, as interpreted by our perception of reflected images. If our care-givers are compassionate, we take on an impression of ourselves as belonging in the world. If dispassion is reflected, we take on a mistrusting nature. This is distal proximal identity (the looking-glass-self) and it works for us in our state of infancy. Pseudo-imprinting is reversible. Man can pseudo-imprint on extraneous impressions the rest of his life and, in fact, there are those who believe mental health is based on the ability to pseudo-imprint what is presented at a given time. They imply that one identify with family, school, baseball team, etc. This misunderstood process also compels some to identify

IDENTIFICATION

with gangs (skinheads), alcohol, guns, etc.

After the upper portions of the brain develop, we learn to conceptualize. Our 'opinion of who we are' becomes hard-coded in our circuitry. Many people retain this form of identity, and it suffices as long as it is not challenged. However, this pseudo-imprinting requires continual legitimazation. We are constantly seeking recognition and approval from a 'peer group'. We see this as distal proximal development (outside in). It has some benefits, but it carries with it the danger of thinking like the crowd.

Since the body organs develop proximal distal (inside out) it only seems logical that our 'mind' should develop proximal distal. To be **mentally** reborn is to imprint on the Spirit within (our sense of being). True imprinting is irreversible. Imprinting the Spirit is the only reality in this life. It is the only entity that will positively be with us till death and perhaps beyond. Training is required for people to acquire values, but when they understand that existence precedes essence, their life is legitimatized. They no longer exist as the looking glass-self. They take control of their lives and allow the inner 'gyroscope' to guide.

Much has been written to describe how conflicts arise when man, lacking true definition, uses contrived methods to protect his fictitious being. One problem has been that each writer is describing the same phenomena with different terminology. Berne called it "the games people play"; Wetherill called it "motives"; Redfield referred to "control drama", etc. All of these methods are used to acquire external energy while a proper definition could show how to attain pure *inner* energy.

Chapter IX

BEHAVIOR

In the past, it was believed that we were born with a conscience; a built in voice that always knew right from wrong. All that was required was to obey it. Since we have discovered that we only get the hardware (synapses) for the brain and not the software (instructions), we must realize we cannot rely on nature to control us as it rules animals.

Human behavior is learned. As stated before, organisms respond to what the environment expects. However, with the freedom of the synapses, man can override what is expected. He can also misunderstand what is expected. He has a propensity to behave in ways that increase his sense of existence. His fantasies are more exciting than his truths. His anticipation is greater than his realization. Why is this?

We know that the brain is designed to function more efficiently in reality. The normal state of the synapses and circuits is firing and resting, in rhythmic patterns. Those who live outside of themselves agitate this pattern. Electro-chemical juice is increased and the person experiences higher states of consciousness. I am told that there is greater anxiety while awaiting to parachute jump than while actually jumping. This is because a mental rehearsal, of what could happen, creates more agitation to the synapses than the reality of the jump.

We can understand most behavior from this vantage point. Much of what we do is to prove our existence. External existence requires more and more ways to increase the flow of endorphins, and behavior can only be partially controlled by external laws.

Behavior that is controlled from within is real to the brain. Fewer chemicals are released and a more sedate emotion is experienced. A person feels more secure because the sense of being is real and constant. This person does not vacillate with relative surroundings. One who senses the Spirit within is no longer swayed by negative peer groups. External law is now secondary because this person can be depended on to follow the natural laws of goodness.

In medicine, it is a mistake to put all of our resources in the study of diseases. It is a mistake in the behavioral sciences to study only aberrations. Tomorrow's nano-technological medical research will learn the structure of a healthy cell. With that information, 'designer molecules' will learn to restore a cell to health, even if an unknown disease invades it. We should follow this lead in the behavioral sciences. We should learn more about **natural laws** of behavior, and understand 'in fact', what makes virtuous people. The attempt to learn why people become corrupt is far more complicated and hopeless than understanding and training people to become righteous (overperson).

Chapter X

UNIVERSAL CONSCIOUSNESS

The Einstein principle of natural laws in nature states that, when we learn to understand truth, it is "simple and beautiful." Before we understood blood circulation, it was seen as mysterious and no doubt incomprehensible. Today, most school children understand the rhythmic flow of blood and how the pump works. There is a universal natural law of mentality that, someday, will be as well-known as blood circulation.

To understand the natural law of consciousness, we can borrow from Einstein's theory of relativity. We seem to be standing still because everything around us is spinning at the same speed. Our earth is spinning at about 1,000 miles per hour while traveling 66,000 mph around the sun. A car at 55 mph is going 67,055 mph depending on our point of reference. Everyone knows the example of standing on the platform watching a train pull out. At times, we have the sensation that we are moving and the train is standing still. A similar relative event occurs in thinking and can be demonstrated [Appendix II].

When one has pseudo-imprinted on an appendage and someone else on another, there is no point of reference. In this setting, communication is based on "motives." How can one communicate when traveling on different points of reference? Even if two people pseudo-imprint on religion, one will accept one version and the other another version. It is an attempt to see the same image by viewing two different pictures. We must understand the spin of 'beliefs' in order to construct a sane universal society. Our beliefs cannot be based on identifying with images. The beginning point to unite us is knowing that the same power energizes all of us. The beginning point is knowing that all synapses are created equal; from there we embark on a distorted journey.

Observing Hitler's psychosis gives us the best vantage point. Why is it that a psychotic leader is reveled while your psychotic neighbor is locked up? It is one thing for an individual to believe his own lies, but how can an entire nation share the lie? Nazism is still alive in the world today. Folie a deux is two people sharing the same psychosis; Nazism is folie a personas, many sharing the same psychosis. The cause is in 'cultural relativity'. Hitler created a national ethos of illness, and since most people take their identity from their frame of reference (external cues) they began to believe his psychosis to be their reality. It was 'collective psychosis'. Those young people who were developing engrams, at the time, could only pseudo-imprint on what was reflected to them. Even today in other countries, we see this genocide by a 'superrace'. How can we know that there is a 'spin' outside of our frame of reference? How can we know that the environment we are responding to is healthy?

A universal formula for mental health is imperative. Consciousness is universal; synapse action is universal. There is a universal natural law for the brain circuits and molecular structures. The first thing that is apparent is that the structure of imprinting *who we are* cannot be left to local perception. A universal formula needs to be based on sound natural laws. Centuries ago Marcus Aurelius said that, "Man must be buttressed from within else his temple crumbles." The same light shines within all human beings and this light is the guiding light of relativity. With a formula for normalcy, we can learn to recognize the light.

The inner core (soul) of each person is identical. This is the basis for teaching universal consciousness. If this inner magnet were understood and accepted, as we accept gravity, the personal *responsibility* for not dimming or snuffing out another's light would be stronger than written law. While the natural law of identity is being understood and digested, we could also use nano-technology to learn how new methods of living affect our synapses. By knowing the true state of a neuron, we can enhance the kinds of behavior that contributes to the health of the neuron. Someday, we will be able to establish bench marks in behavior as we have in the physical body; i.e. body temperature, blood pressure, etc.

People would strive for emotional health if they had a definition of emotional health. They now strive to maintain physical health because they know the definition of physical health. People would strive to become 'overperson', by following natural laws of behavior, if a logical set of instructions (owner's manual) were devised. We are now at a stage of "Homo ignoramus" (Velikovsky's term) but we will soon evolve to 'Homo overperson' (my term). The Second Coming...?

An important step in implementing the Second Coming is to internalize Jesus' message on his first visit. In his time, knowledge and power were controlled by a few. Those in power attempted to keep

UNIVERSAL CONSCIOUSNESS 45

everyone ignorant in order to maintain control. Enter Jesus who said, "The Spirit is within you," and you are free to learn the truth of the world. Your allegiance should be to the Spirit. Think of the money lost by those in power when people no longer had to pay for forgiveness. He was a loose cannon wandering over the countryside. Of course he had to die! Pseudo-powerful people identify with extrinsic appendages (false gods) and, even today, the only way they can deal with a threat, to their tenuous existence, is to destroy the threat.

We surely can agree that the Spirit of God was alive in the universe at the beginning. Prior to Jesus there were those who understood the Spirit. He (and others) refocused the message and explained that your *sins* (stupid acts) dissolve when you focus on Spiritual energy (imprint the Spirit). He explained that we should not make graven images or make sacrifices. How then, in the name of enlightenment, can we say that God would sacrifice one of his sons for our sins? The mechanism for forgiveness was already in place.

The Christ principle was alive in the world all along. The 'Christ principle' is to live your life knowing that the Spirit is within. Jesus had embodied the Christ. He knew the Son of God (Spirit) was in Him, and he merely wanted to share "the good news" that we are all sons and daughters of God. In an effort by some to remain in control after Jesus, a myth was concocted to assure control by manning the 'toll booth to Heaven'. Electricity was electricity before we understood it. Gravity functioned the same before Jesus. The Spirit is the same now as it was before Jesus. Did gravity only begin to work when we finally understood it; does it now only work for a select few? Jesus changed no Spiritual natural law; He only showed us how to fulfill it.

It takes an overperson to accept the reality that the Spirit is present in *all,* because it means that no nation or denomination has the only key. It means that everyone experiences the Spirit, and that a part of all of us is immortal. In George G. Ritchie's compelling book, *Return from Tomorrow,* he believed that the "light" was Jesus. As I read his book, I did not find where the light made that inference. This seemed to be Dr. Ritchie's level of understanding which was allowed to stay with him. He later states that "The more I learned to see 'Christ' in other people...." It is interesting that he did not say "in other Christians." The **CHRIST** (Spirit) is in all people and is seen when the carrier allows it to shine. Ritchie wrote that, after death, cruel people continued to suffer at the hands of other cruel beings until they became aware of the light. Maybe the saying "we reap what we sow" means, we reap in the *next plane* what we sow in this one.

Chapter XI

LOVE

Love is the feeling we feel, just before we feel the feeling, we have never felt before. Love is one of the most misunderstood and misused words in our language. In the Sixties we were told, "Aggression will go away if we just 'love' everyone." Apply large doses of 'love potion' unilaterally and it will heal despicable acts. Fascists and communists thrived on that practice because they interpreted it as weakness. Had that solution been applied to Hitler, we would all be goose-stepping today. However, there is a force in the world called 'love' but, for it to have meaning and power, it must be better understood. It must be definable.

Tropism is the force that is alive in nature. It is the cybernetic force that guides a moth to a light bulb at night. Love is as definable a force in humans except our free will allows us to interfere with its symmetry. The light (Spirit) is in every human and we would be attracted to it if we dropped our appendages (virtual realities).

Love is the recognition of the flow of energy in others. Our love for others should be seen as a pooling of Spiritual energy. The ultimate attraction is the Superlight (God).

Love has many disguises. If real love could be understood and practiced bilaterally, disguised love would vanish. False love has been around for such a long time that some can no longer distinguish it from real love. False love is an attempt to sap energy, by manipulation, from another being. Spiritual energy is complete. The 'O's on the book cover represent this wholeness. Those who are not aware of the energy are like a 'C' (Redfield). They compete for this energy, and are trying to complete the circle by siphoning it from another. The human brain is a closed energy field and 'sparking-over' (conflict) occurs when competing. It is a law that we cannot acquire our energy from another. Love is sensing and sharing the higher energy source as opposed to an attempt to acquire each other's energy. Marriage for the sole purpose of completing the 'C' disrupts the energy field and usually fails. Marriage of two 'O's usually lasts for a lifetime.

Marriage courses teach that *romantic* love is the glue that keeps two people together while they adjust to each other's ways. Marriage brings the word 'mirage' to mind in that certain negative behaviors are overshadowed at first. Romantic love might not be love at all but rather a chemical reaction to a new experience. A roller coaster ride supplies the same adrenaline rush except the thrill subsides quicker. Today, many marriages take on the characteristics of a roller coaster ride.

Immature love is coercive. It stems from childhood methods of attaining love by holding one's breath or beating the spoon on the highchair. Lying, cheating and stealing can be spin-offs of this practice. It is an ill conceived method of attaining temporary emotional security. Immature love is disguised as favors with strings attached. The implication is, if you fulfill my needs (energy field) I will continue to 'love' you. Usually one has trouble knowing what those needs are. Withholding love is a weapon that often misfires.

Neurotic love is the most destructive. At first neurotic love appears to be the 'real thing'. We see parents who give up everything for their child and we hear, "They really love that child." In reality it might be neurotic identification empathy. The parents might be reliving their empty lives through the child, and the child's success is really vicarious success for the parents. This does untold damage to the child, most of which can only be seen in later life. Of course, mentally healthy, loving people enjoy the successes of their children or friends, but they do not *become* the successes.

Sexual love, too, is subjective. Freud is said to have supported the idea that most social problems are due to the suppression of sexual desires. However, now some people believe that there was confusion in translation. The term might have been *sensual,* which falls under the autotelic principle. There is an observable desire in human beings to fulfill an expression of the senses. We build magnificent buildings, paint beautiful pictures and compose an endless array of music. There is a natural law that great satisfaction is derived from new learning and discovery. Suppressed *sensual* desires would make more sense because man does have a propensity to create. If this creativity is blocked, one could suffer emotionally. The inconsistency in believers of frustrated sexual desires is interesting. They insist that people become criminals or experience emotional turmoil because of suppressed sex, but their recommended treatment is to *lock them up* which only exacerbates the situation. It would seem more prudent to furnish these people with unbridled sex. The cure, of course, is to teach the deviant that sex is an appendage. As in any addiction, imprinting on *reality* controls the dependency.

One can find a false identity in sex. In some, it becomes *who they are* just as an alcoholic finds solace in alcohol. Of course, the difference is that sex is more socially accepted because it can be disguised as *love*. Rape and sexual assaults are the result of reinforcing an appendage. This action falls in the forth and fifth order of dyscontrol.

Why does one 'love' members of their own sex? The answer is complex. Except in rare cases, it has more to do with a comfort zone than genes. It has been shown that certain kinds of child-rearing practices contribute to the confusion. If one finds less of a threat in dealing with someone within one's own sex, the 'feeling' can be misinterpreted as love. We have talked about the androgynous Spirit which resides in male and female. We can appreciate the Spirit in others of our sex, but constructing an appendage, or pseudo-imprinting on our same sex is the *misuse* of Spiritual energy.

Someone has said, "Love is deoxyribonucleic acid (DNA) crying out to itself." At least this is a step in the right direction. There must be a base line in order to grasp pure love; it cannot be 'just what anybody thinks'. It should be something real that we can observe and depend on just as we do electricity. There is a particle rhythm that occurs in real love. Most people agree that love is a mood altering agent. Why should this be? The brain's mission in life is to seek cognitive symmetry. Spiritual energy is about as symmetric as symmetry can get. When we allow ourselves to sense this energy flowing through our brain, we experience a comforting and soothing sensation. This is God's (Spirit) unconditional love which we should emulate. It is there in each of us to adore and to experience, and cannot be taken away. It is limitless! It is agape!

When we sense comfort in the Spirit in others, is it not the communion of spiritual symmetry? When others allow this light to shine, does it not permeate the spirituality of all? Someday, real love will register on a meter just as a pure musical note can now be confirmed by a tuning fork. Real love sets up a resonance that is as sure as the distribution of electrons in atoms, and gives rise to stabilization of a structure.

One must distinguish between excitement of the synapses and love. When one is neurotically attached to another, one can receive a love-like feeling. One can *feel love* when sharing another's appendages. This can be seen as infatuation and can fool people into thinking they are 'in love'. This is pseudo-love and, for the most part, these are the kinds of marriages we have seen in the divorce crazed years. This is the kind of love one 'falls out of' because appendages are unstable and dissolve under pressure. One explanation for society's turmoil is that, as consciousness evolves, it moves to the forefront. Appendages can no longer be used as an identity, and we have not yet learned to cope with reality. It is as though *superperson* is covertly evolving.

Real love is the core of the Spirit crying out to itself. It is unconditional and unchanging. When one imprints on the Spirit within, unconditional love is the only kind of love that one would know. Motives and appendages will lose their dominance and assume their proper roles.

Can love cure the world? **Real** love can! We need not isolate the reasons people are hateful, cruel, greedy and vicious. All we need to know is that every human being has a Spirit that is seeking recognition and reunion. How can one hate another knowing the Spirit is alive in that person whether that person knows it or not? How can we be cruel to another and try to dim each others *light* if we know the light is THE CHRIST? Greed vanishes when man builds on cognitive symmetry (love) as opposed to building a fortune. Ugly acts are man's inventions brought about by attempting to defend phony beliefs and identities.

Chapter XII

MEDITATION

Meditation and group therapy are contrived ways of eliminating layers of thought that have alienated people from themselves. Dr. Jon Kaabat-Zinn in Bill Moyer's book *Healing and the Mind* said, "Here we focus on who you are as a human being...to bring you into the present moment" and "give the mind one thing to concentrate on." Dr. John Zawacki, in the same book states, "I think they tap into some portion of themselves (in meditation) that they didn't know they had and that we probably all have." It requires years to attempt to find the *true* person inside by identifying false appendages outside. It is a never-ending exercise. Many times, when one appendage is eliminated, another fills its place. It is like the alcoholic who replaces alcohol with the group meeting. Of course, the meeting is more socially accepted, but the subject is still pseudo-imprinting on something unreal.

It is possible to identify 'that portion' of themselves (Spirit-titre) by learning how to *experience* their consciousness. When this occurs, the exercise of eliminating motives is unnecessary.

There are those who fear their own body. They hesitate learning how it functions for fear it is sacred or beyond their comprehension. Some never look inward into their secret world for fear there is something sinister in there. There is nothing in there except the Spirit (the sense of being) and what we put in there. To the contrary, the only thing to fear is the *unwillingness* to locate the inner self.

Therapy would be less time consuming, and more effective, if we would start by identifying what we wish to accomplish. If one can begin by locating pure reality, virtual reality falls into place. Appendages no longer own the client and he/she no longer must deal with them one at a time. Biofeedback does not eliminate motives, it simply registers on the dial when the subject attains some sort of inner symmetry. After the training, the person is expected to be able to acquire symmetry at will. Of course, this is beneficial but the client often does not understand the process that is taking place. The symmetry does not become a part of their character structure.

We have found immortality when we know that cosmic energy particles are igniting our sense of consciousness. It does not need to be reinforced daily. *Faith* is not required in order to experience the energy. It becomes a part of our character structure and we live life from a new perspective. One might choose to meditate but not in an effort to find oneself. Meditation need only be practiced in order to *magnify* the inner Spirit.

Many forms of meditation suggest that we focus our mind on one thought (mantra). This helps but it is an external experience. Some suggest that we concentrate on breathing. This seems to suffice, but sensing air entering and leaving the body is actually *not* sensing the Spiritual presence. To sense the soul, one has to experience the energy particles entering the lower brain which activates our arousal centers. In a sense it is like breathing. We are taking forms of subatomic energy particles into the lower brain, metabolizing them into body energy and storing them in memory traces. The efficacy of this process is that we have an awareness of the 'engine' running. The *awareness* is the sixth sense (consciousness).

There is a tangible explanation why it is beneficial to locate the center of one's being. We now know that there are transmitters and receptors in both the brain and the body, particularly in the immune system. If one's circuits are scattered and busy searching for meaning in extrinsic images, this causes spill-over. Some people's thoughts reach into fantasies which cause more disruption. All of this overload interferes with the mind/body connection which requires symmetry in order for the busy little atoms to do what they are supposed to do. We can think of the mind/body as atomic tides. We have proof of this because we see the effect of the moon on some people's *tides* just as we observe ocean tides. When tides are normal, there is a rhythmic beat. When we allow ourselves to entertain disruptive thoughts, the rhythmic swells are disturbed and it forces some atoms to swim against the tide. In time the disequilibrium of the cells causes them to break down. Mental well-being is dynamic energy flowing to the beat of the 'atomic drum'.

We need to gain control of our thoughts. We control the brain; it does not control us. This is critical to our well-being. Not because it is logical but because it is a natural law. The Spirit must be recognized and allowed to express its being. The body *becomes* what the mind thinks it is. The mind is capable of causing an organ to do anything that the organ is capable of doing. If the mind is cluttered and thinks that the body is ill, the body will become ill. Even the act of attempting to 'will' oneself well can interfere with the natural flow. A collected mind can be attained by imprinting on the Spirit within. Imprinting causes atomic symmetry; then the body is *compelled* to become healthy, unless there is organ damage. Cognitive consonance results by focusing on the center, and this promotes the "peace that passeth all understanding." The sense of inner security allows symmetry among the transmitters and receptors and eventually health materializes. It is a natural law.

Since the body unwittingly responds to the *mind's ideas*, the body assumes features of these ideas, provided the ideas remain within the realm of the organisms natural laws. If we formulate an idea that our body is ill, either by accommodation or disruption of molecular symmetry, we become ill. This also implies that a male could think *female* and the body would display effeminate traits. The irony is, these thoughts might synthesize female juices and, when tested, would suggest that the female juices caused the effeminate traits.

It is important to emphasize that by law an organ can only do what the organ was coded to do. Mankind has *never* witnessed a supernatural event. Even near death experiences follow natural law. As miraculous as they are, they remain within the guidelines of the particle theory.

If an organ is permanently damaged, there is no recovery regardless of 'visualization'. We have never seen a human limb grow back (except by surgical reattachment). Perhaps this rebuilding could become a reality in the age of 'cell manufacturing'.

Stress reduction and meditation programs are good for the economy but many people cannot afford such luxuries. Why do we need an expensive program to elicit the energy that God has already provided? We feel that someone else must intercede for us; someone must do it for us. We *need* to be a victim. Is it too simple to say that the mind and body are one? 'Sensing the moment' is to sense the Spiritual energy within which allows a synergism of cells beyond belief. This has nothing to do with 'willing' oneself well; it has to do with creating the conditions that *allow* one to be well.

Society is confused about healing. It is generally divided into two camps; religious healing that many times borders on fantasy, and medicine which does not always have the desired effect. In both of these examples, there is usually a middle person who likes to be paid. Both camps are equally important but ultimately one's own mind/body must do the healing. The more one is involved in the equation, the better. Sometimes medicine provides a needed boost, but often the mind/body recovers without medicine. One who lives in reality requires fewer boosts.

The Spirit does not come down from on high to heal, as some believe. IT does not rearrange your cells. The power already dwells within and, by mental change, cells are allowed to repair themselves. Faith healers do nothing to heal. It is your own mind set that brings about any change. Perhaps they change your mind about something but you alone control the cells of your body. Except for accidents or physical contacts with disease (even then, in some instances, we can suspect the mind) body change takes place by what is already coded in the molecular atoms. This does not require a middle person. The natural law of healing is implicit in this understanding. It does not depend on one's doctrine or faith. If the mind/body can attain the proper symmetry, healing occurs to the just and unjust alike.

Of course, we need others for our physical well-being, but we are on shaky ground when adults look to others for emotional stability. The crux of group therapy is the attention one receives. It pseudo-validates one's being; it affords recognition and self-worth. It can also form another false image. Is it not the purpose of therapy to remove false images?

Chapter XIII

VANISHING TRIBES

During my 'age of enlightenment' at the University of Pittsburgh, one of my professors said that, "Psychology is a vanishing tribe." Since then, the truth in that statement has become apparent to me. Except for organic causes (which are few) mental illness is merely straying from reality. In the real *Second Coming,* men and women will understand reality and teach it to their children. There will be no need for counseling in order to find reality. There will be no fantasy except at Disney World. The name of this chapter is plural because during the *Second Coming* there will be many vanishing tribes.

By that time, we will have discovered "gene readers" and "cell manufacturing." The billions of dollars that we now spend on disease research, will be used to directly regenerate cell structures. It will be the ultimate in specialization. Instead of heart, lung, or brain specialists, etc., we will have the 'cell specialist' who will repair a cell, regardless of what disease caused the damage.

We will no longer 'live for winning the lotto' but will live in an understanding of the Spirit. We will not need to send donations to TV evangelists, pay big fees to psychiatrists or lawyers, etc. We will not need law enforcement or jails. We will use those billions to help people who obey written laws instead of wasting it on those who disobey them, as we do now. If the timing of the *Coming* is right, we can use part of these savings to maintain senior citizens. By then there will be fewer young people to support the aged, because Social Security will have been squandered by devious politicians.

Recently, Dr. Allen J. Francis and his colleagues have updated the *Diagnostic and Statistical Manual of Mental Disorders*. In 1987 the manual contained 292 disorders and they have since added eight more. What a travesty! None of this attempts to define *sanity*. As in religion, we use anti-logic, we attempt to locate good by identifying and attacking evil. Can we determine what sanity is by defining insanity? It seems more realistic to isolate the *one* characteristic *sanity* rather than determine *hundreds* of insane traits, which often are altered by whomever makes the determination.

Many years ago, Dr. Menninger discovered the wisdom in identifying sanity. He introduced the idea that all mental disorders stem from one source. All of the "pigeon hole" names psychiatrists give to disorders serve no purpose. If all of the *learned* people would put their efforts into describing *normal* it would, first, present a model for those who strive for normalcy and, second, supply a simple graph to diagnose those who fall short. The first order of dyscontrol would be residing in reality and understanding virtual reality. The second order would be vacillating between reality and virtual reality. The third order would exist in virtual reality and function on the fringe of society. The fourth order would be losing touch with reality and becoming a danger to oneself. The fifth order migrates to 'never never' land and is a danger to society. These parameters would be easy to establish and monitor.

Would this hold up in court? In a murder case, it would be simpler for the prosecutor to state, "This person falls into the fifth order of dysfunction." Would that not be more informative than bringing in the 'experts', who disagree among themselves, explaining the defendant is a manic-depressive sociopath with paranoid tendencies, because his hobby horse died when he was young?

Chapter XIV

THE REAL SECOND COMING

Jesus said, "Think not that I am come to destroy the law...." The intent of this book is not to destroy the myth of external law, but to promote the understanding of natural law. Natural law has little to do with what God expects. It has little to do with the Ten Commandments or the Sermon on the Mount. It has least to do with what we *think* is right. "Which of you by taking thought can add one cubit unto his stature?" Which of us, by *thinking* we can do what we want, escapes the natural law already in motion? Natural law is alive in the universe and follows the natural law of "logical consequences." God has given us the power and the authority to do what needs to be done, but we are waiting for Jesus or others to do it. What needs to be done is to be cognitive of the sixth sense (Spirit) and the role it plays on the other five.

We can preach the evils of alcohol and drugs but, whether the message is heard or believed, these chemicals do permanent damage to synapses (brain cells). Telling someone that certain behavior is wrong usually has the opposite effect. The thrill of disobedience overshadows the purpose. We waste our time explaining *wrong behavior*. We should develop a universal ethos of what is *right behavior*. People need to know what the consequences are when they do not adhere to natural law. One example is, destroyed brain cells (who among us can spare any) are the consequence of excessive drink whether the alcoholic believes it or not.

THE REAL SECOND COMING 63

We pass written laws against drunk driving to stop needless killing, but it does not stop the slaughter. When one is in the *fantasy land* of drink, the law against driving loses its authority. As a child, if one learns what true security is would one require appendages? We agree with a good friend who has suggested that "A meteor would strike the earth before we learn to grasp this truth", but let sanity begin today and "let it begin with us."

Fascism, a more serious affliction than drugs, is alive today. We have failed to teach the commonalty of what it is to be human. One would expect that, since the world calamity of Hitler, we would have learned to deal with this plague. Fascism is the direct result of promoting the idea in young people to pseudo-imprint on nationality and race. The natural law states that, when one identifies with something unreal, one will go to any length to protect and enhance that false identity. People who live in a constant state of insecurity are capable of ruthless behavior. Ruthless behavior is the logical consequence of worshiping idols (appendages).

There may be no cure in this world for the affliction of false identity; the solution is to prevent its development. Everything in the universe functions like a solar system. Even the little atom has a nucleus that holds it together. A human is no different, except we have attained the *right* to decide not to be *held together*. Our nucleus is the Spirit within. It is our sense of existence. When we begin to believe we are the extrinsic particles (appendages) instead of the nucleus, we fly apart. This is not just someone's idea; we have seen the consequences of disregarding this law for those using drugs or practicing a Fascist political system. This cancer of insecurity affects the lives of all of us. These people are in the third or fourth order on the 'spiritual influence table'.

We can squander money on treaties and world courts, or we can use that money to study the natural law of human behavior (inner self, God particle). We can use that money to spread the news to the world that all human beings are powered by the same energy. The proper use of that energy is the Second Coming and would produce a world of *overpersons*. The Real Second Coming will occur when we understand and follow the natural laws of behavior. Those who follow these laws will exist in the first order of 'The Spiritual Influence Table'.

Chapter XV

PROPHESY

It seems as though God should check with 'predictors' in order to know how to plan the future. The first thing that should come to mind to those engaged in the prophesy *business* is that it negates free will. If the future is already determined, then why not just sit back and let it happen? Let us forget the purpose of the frontal lobe and pretend we are robots playing out the *Big Guy's* hand.

Prediction flourishes because we distrust the unknown. Predictions, even when bad, give order to one's life. When a prediction comes to pass, that event is seized upon and deified. It does not seem to matter how many predictions do not come to pass, people continue to be fascinated by predictions. It is difficult to give up a comfortable fantasy. Cause and effect are difficult to prove. As mentioned before, if a bird chirps out in the yard and a chair falls over, we can claim the bird's chirp caused the chair to fall. Reality should tell us to gather more evidence; we would need to see this happen *every* time the bird chirped. We can predict with certainty what happens when natural laws are disobeyed; i.e., jumping from a tenth-story balcony because we think we can fly. We can predict with some certainty that the sun will come up tomorrow because it obeys natural laws. Predictions based on natural laws are the only ones that are factual.

What does prediction prove? How does it strengthen any cause? Does it make God *more* or *less* for us to "predict" what He is going to do? Is everybody suddenly going to be on their best behavior if they hear the world is ending? These predictors lose credibility when HE fails to meet their deadline. The first *rule of hole,* when you are in one, is to stop digging. These folks continue to dig deeper.

Since man learned that nothing happens in the universe except by natural events, it would seem advantageous to learn more about natural events. We know that if we heat water to a certain degree it will boil. The water atoms do what they were 'wired' to do. We know that if a fault line attains enough strain, the atoms on the earth plates will lose their ability to bond and an earthquake will occur. We know that if human beings endure emotional stress long enough, their immune system atoms will collapse. These examples are not prophesies; they are the result of observing recurring phenomena and applying physics.

All events turn out to be natural when they are proven and understood. These natural occurrences are awesome when we consider the billions of atoms involved and how many of these tiny particles must hit their 'target' for the event to materialize. It would seem anticlimactic to think the occurrence could be more awesome because someone 'predicted' they would happen. Man's position in the universe is tenuous at best. Promoting the belief that his life is already preordained removes his *responsibility* for improvement.

There are enough variables out of our control without giving up and saying, "What will be, will be." There is little incentive for mankind to responsibly mature when it shares the belief that somewhere there is a 'great plan' and that only a few have privilege to it. The 'great plan' is already in effect in the photon action of the atom. It is our *responsibility* to learn how natural law works. We are waiting for something to light our fire, and it is already lit.

Until now, we have talked about the Spiritual particles dwelling in our body, but purposefully we have not discussed divine guidance. It would seem that if God's Spirit is a part of us this would be our guidance system. It is tempting to buy into this idea, and many do, but again we must respect the natural law of free will. If God would give us the inside track on investments or lottery numbers, it would negate our free will. It would also be impossible to separate which messages come from *Her* and which are our own. If there are authentic messages, how can one distinguish between those and the "Son of Sam" messages?

The Spirit is alive in the universe but It only provides raw energy. We can do with It what we will. The gasoline in the automobile does not guide the auto to its proper destination. The only direction provided by the Spirit is the particle action. We need to understand the trajectory of atoms and clusters of atoms as they obey their preprogrammed instructions.

Today the magic term is 'visualize'. To visualize something is to make it come true. Of course, right thinking causes symmetry of atoms and molecules. It allows healing and well-being to occur, but one must guard against over-sell. We see the golfer visualize the shot but the ball flies in the direction it was hit. Everything must follow its natural law. An interesting experiment would be to visualize a wrecker when one's auto is broken down out on the desert.

Chapter XVI

GOD'S WILL

It is presumptuous to pretend to 'know the will of God', yet we hear it practiced daily. We hear that, "God wanted me to get the raise", "God wanted me to get well" and, in death, it was "God's will."

What in the world is the will of God? It has to be based more on fact than on our subjective interpretation. Please stay with me on this one. The 'will of God' was in power before the creation. The specifications were already in place. This is the only logical explanation of the *profound order* in the universe. The creating explosion was totally orderly and its path predictable even though it followed the uncertainty principle. Life itself is the result of continual, somewhat predictable, explosions. The universe is made up of particles following their built-in instructions (the will of God?). The Higgs particles (smaller than those that scientists have, so far, been able to demonstrate) are constantly firing in the universe and also in our brain as 'nano-matchheads'.

Before we leave the creating explosion idea, think for a minute about the world having no beginning and no end. The human brain cannot fathom something having no beginning. Applying the big bang cycle, no beginning and no end takes on new understanding. If particles collapse or implode into themselves (black hole, decay) then explode (big bang, seed) and expand (red shift, flowering) this self-perpetuating cycle would need no beginning and no end.

Mankind's most important revelation will come when we finally realize that God's will is understandable in human terms. God's will is simply the process (by grand design) of atoms being attracted and repulsed with a purpose. God's will is quantum mechanics. The greatest of all revelations will remove regional and personal multi-Gods. The result will be universal understanding and will bring mankind under *one* Spiritual roof. The only demonstrable and dependable force in the universe is the relation of particles to each other (God's will).

We have searched for definitions of a God *out there,* but they have not revealed a definable force. We have studied artifacts. They tell us a great deal, but again no great definable force is revealed. The answer turns out to be *in there.* By observing the predictable forces of the most minuscule particle, we *can* understand natural laws that govern the universe (God's will).

Nothing has ever happened in the universe that was not the direct result of subatomic explosions. The 'miracle' of these explosions is that, as random as they seem, enough particles hit their target to promote order as opposed to chaos. If it were any other way we could not exist. For instance, if gravity were directed from *above,* a certain type airplane might take off at 80 mph one time and 120 mph another. Sometimes an acorn might develop into an apple tree; a chick might crawl back into its shell. There is always structural improvement. Occasionally an asteroid runs amok, but enough explosions follow their 'instructions' that (so far) we have not seen cosmic destruction. Occasionally, a liver molecule runs amok but, universally, there are billions more that remain intact.

It seems like a pretty good idea to run the universe on energy particles because they regenerate and present a unified pattern. If the mind of God were an on-going thought process it would always leave us guessing. Every time He would change His mind, we would have to rewrite the system. There would be no way for us to know that today fire might burn while tomorrow it might not. Because His energy (the fifth force) follows laws, we can know Its 'will', and if we misuse an atom it is our fault. We can be sure the atom is always perfect. Because it follows laws, we always know how to "return to paradise" (Lederman's phrase) by creating conditions that return our particles to symmetry. We can attain cognitive consonance by recognizing the resonance of the Spiritual particles within.

We have temporarily slowed our understanding of the "God Particle", especially since we have lost the Supercolliding Super Conducting Accelerator Project. We have reached a barrier in discovering the smallest particle (Higgs). This is reminiscent of the sound barrier. There were those who felt that the sound barrier could not or should not be broken. Just as we penetrated the sound barrier, we will penetrate the Higgs barrier. We develop more and more sophisticated apparatus to study the smallest particle, but the closer we get the more elusive it becomes. It is like locating the North Pole; the closer we get, the more diffuse the attraction and the instruments become less dependable. It is like finding the absolute source of a light. It is easy to see the stream of light when standing outside of the beam. As we enter, the beam becomes more diffused; as we continue on into the beam the photons become more and more difficult to identify. It becomes a formidable task to locate the exact source.

There is no *will* telling these particles, "you do this and you do that", as though they were misbehaving children. Instead, the instructions already are 'locked-in'. They are like an accomplished orchestra. For the most part, they can continue 'playing the music' on their own — after the conductor signals them when to start. The universe has always performed this way. Atoms and subatomic particles have never changed, only our understanding of them has changed.

How can we apply these forces in our own lives? First, we need to realize that we have *primary contact* with the Power Source. When we attempt to replace that source with an external source (appendages), we are out of synchronization. It should give us a clue when we begin to look for our strength in things or in other persons, especially in the Mansons or Jonestown Joneses. Growth is halted when one ('C') becomes addicted to capturing energy from an external source. The mind and Spiritual energy are a closed loop ('O'). Consciousness and energy have an *internal* source. Realization and acceptance of this process will unfold the "Second Coming."

NEW TESTAMENT II

You shall know that consciousness is the Spirit *in* man. It is man's immortality.

You shall sense the Spirit within and *It*, first, shall you worship and enhance.

Know that universal energy (first cause) dwells *within*. It is the *one* unified energy field and the prime mover of man, earth, sea and universe. Accept the responsibility for Its use.

You shall glorify the Spirit which is real, and realize that perceptions are graven images.

Know that Spiritual energy exists in *all* human beings, and encourage *Its* flow in others.

Trust the sensed Spirit-center *within* so that the body can attain molecular symmetry.

Honor your caregivers who nurtured you while you were discovering the "Silver cord" of energy.

Help others discover and develop a deep sense of the Spirit that dwells *within* them.

Love the Spirit that inhabits others as you love It in yourself.

Know that, when you live by the principle of right-mindedness, you shall enjoy the rewards: kindness, love, understanding, caring, honesty, harmony, honor and peace.

This is a *works in progress*. Permission is granted to add to this Testament with new, *pure* knowledge and the *latest* scientific discoveries.

REFERENCES

Berra, Tim M.
Evolution and the Myth of Creationism

Bohm, David
Wholeness and the Implicate Order

Carrigan, Richard A. & Tower, W. Peter
Particles and Forces at the Heart of the Matter

Dreikurs, Rudolf M.D. and Loren Grey, Ph.D.
Logical Consequences

Drexler, Eric K.
Engines of Creation

Drexler, Eric K.
Unbounding the Future

Hawking, Steven
A Brief History of Time

Johanson, Donald
ANCESTORS: In Search of Human Origins

Jourard, Sidney M.
The Transparent Self (first edition)

Lederman, Leon
The God Particle

Marrs, Texe
New Age Cults and Religions

Morse, Melvin, M.D., with Paul Perry
Closer to the Light

Moyers, Bill
Healing and the Mind

Redfield, James
The Celestine Prophecy

Ritchie, George G. / Sherrill, Elizabeth
Return From Tomorrow

Rose, Steven
The Making of Memory

Villetto, Reverend Robert
Mind With Reason

Watson, James D.
The Double Helix

Wetherill, Richard W.
Emergence of Rationality (Volume 15)

Zukav, Gary
The Dancing Wu Li Masters (The New Physics)

APPENDIX I

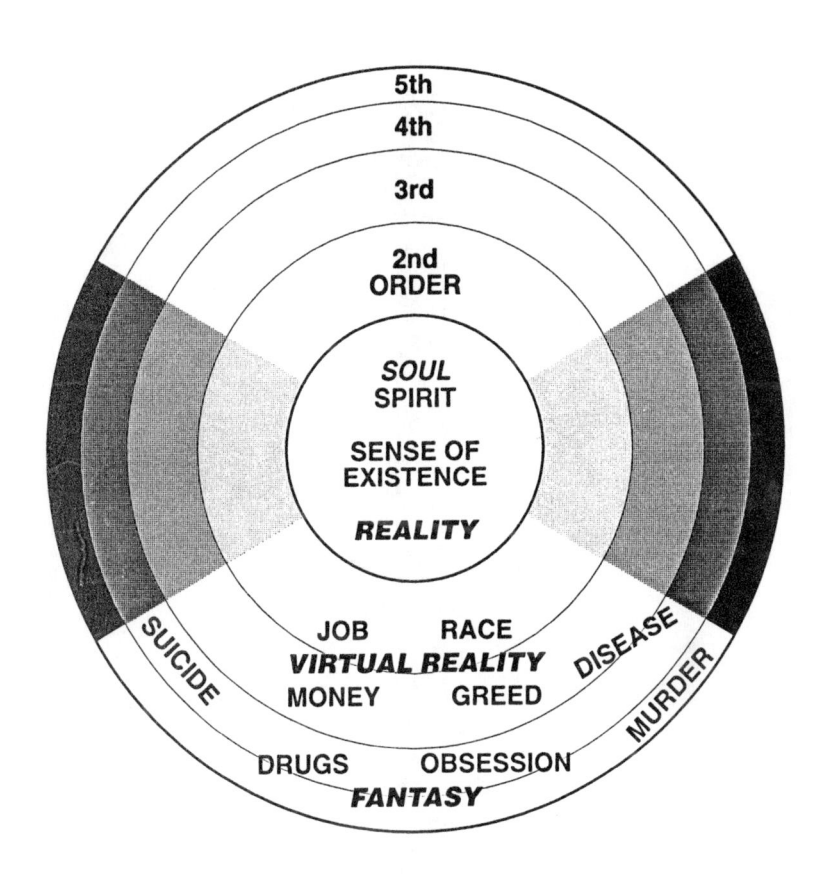

Rings (outer to inner): 5th, 4th, 3rd, 2nd ORDER

Center:
SOUL
SPIRIT
SENSE OF EXISTENCE
REALITY

Lower segment:
JOB   RACE
VIRTUAL REALITY
MONEY   GREED
DRUGS   OBSESSION
FANTASY

Outer segments: SUICIDE, DISEASE, MURDER

"COME OUT OF THE DARKNESS AND INTO THE LIGHT"

APPENDIX II

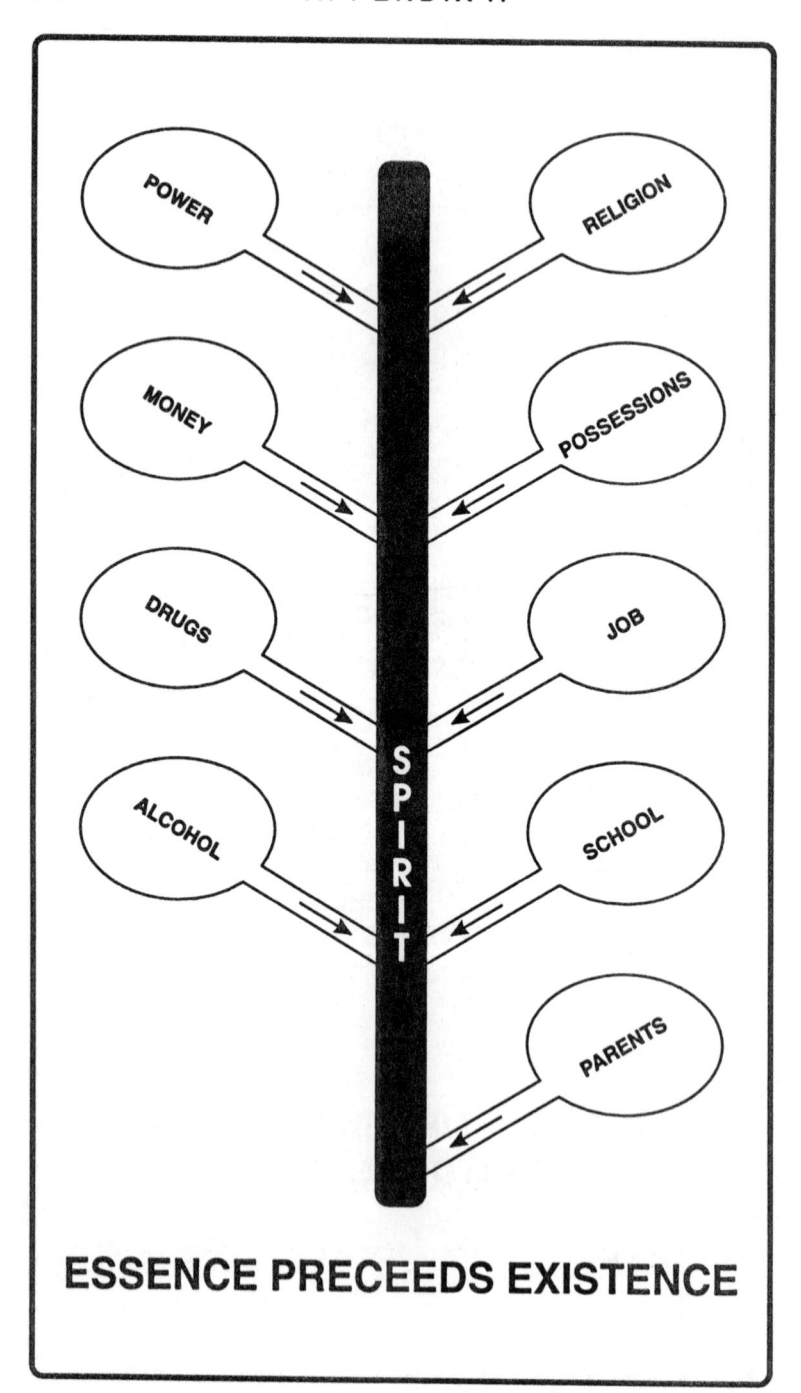

ESSENCE PRECEEDS EXISTENCE

APPENDIX III

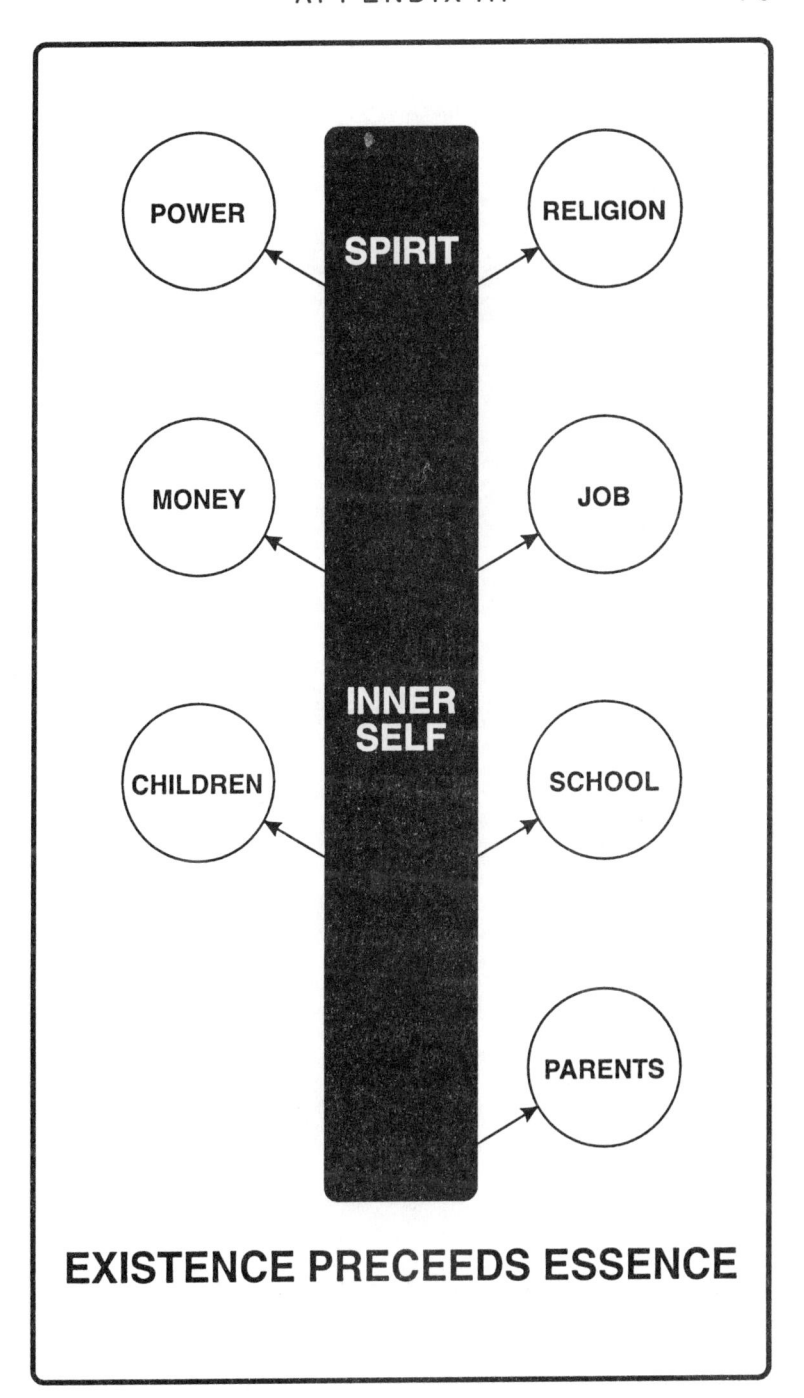

SPIRIT

- POWER
- RELIGION
- MONEY
- JOB

INNER SELF

- CHILDREN
- SCHOOL
- PARENTS

EXISTENCE PRECEEDS ESSENCE

AUTISM

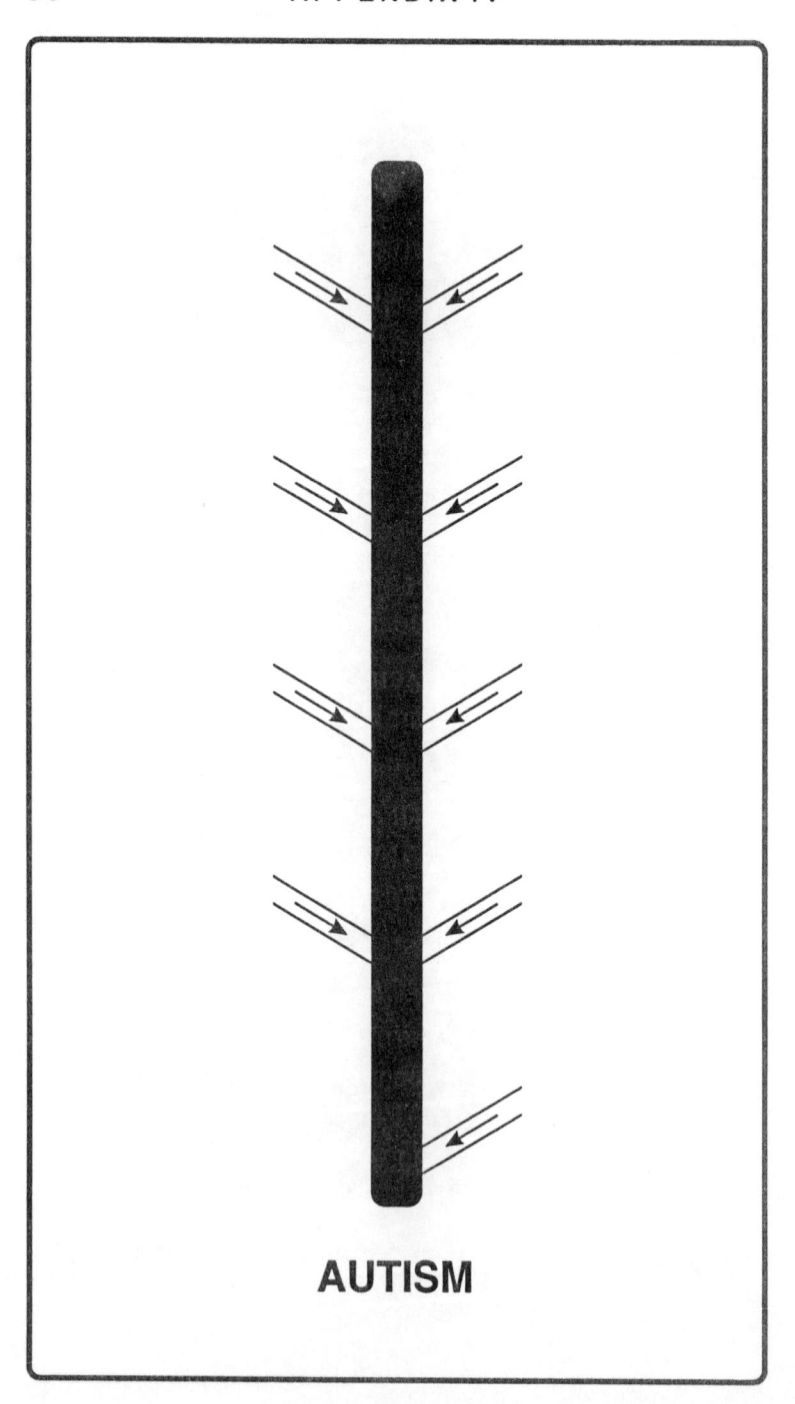

APPENDIX V

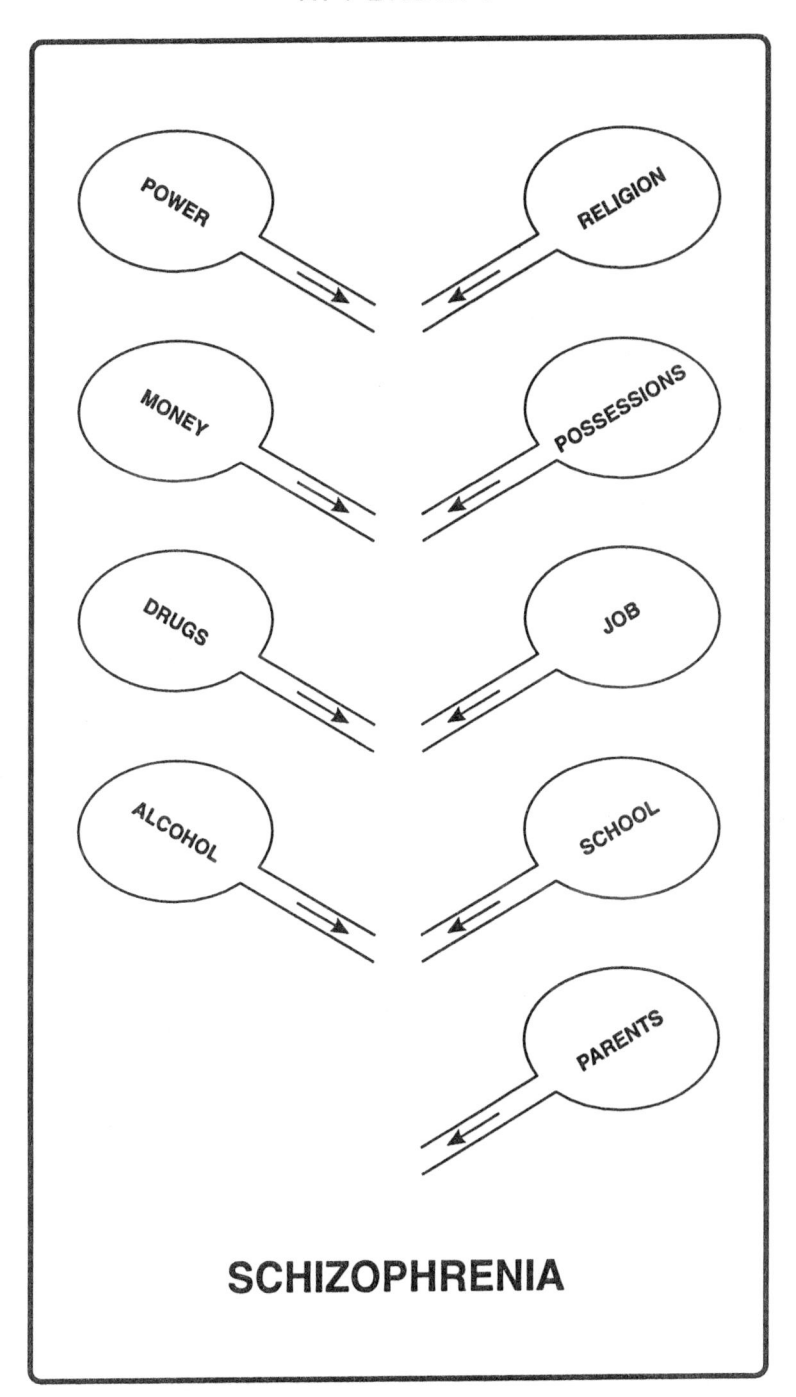

POWER

RELIGION

MONEY

POSSESSIONS

DRUGS

JOB

ALCOHOL

SCHOOL

PARENTS

SCHIZOPHRENIA

— ORDER FORM —
Also available at local bookstores.

QUANTITY

_____ ***THE RISE OF MAN***
_____ ***MAN IS RISEN***
_____ ***UNIVERSAL REALITY***

Please mail the books indicated above to this address:

NAME _____

ADDRESS _____

CITY _____

STATE _____ ZIP _____

NUMBER OF BOOKS ORDERED:

_____ x $5.95 PER BOOK = $ _____

FLA. RESIDENTS ADD 6% SALES TAX
plus, if applicable: YOUR COUNTY SURTAX = $ _____

_____ x $2.00 PER BOOK
FOR POSTAGE & HANDLING = $ _____

TOTAL AMOUNT ENCLOSED = $ _____

*Make Check or Money Order
(no cash or C.O.D.) payable to:*

HAROLD S. COBER
P.O. BOX 4815
SOUTH DAYTONA, FL 32127

Please allow 4 to 6 weeks for delivery. Prices and availability subject to change without notice.